American Pit Bull Terrier

Handbook

Joe Stahlkuppe

BARRON'S

About the Author

Joe Stahlkuppe has written over 25 pet-related books, many hundreds of articles, and hosted and produced several popular radio shows on animals and their people. He lives near Birmingham, Alabama, with his wife of 36 years, with visits from his son Shawn and his pet-loving grandchildren: the actress Cathie Stahlkuppe, the scholar Peter Stahlkuppe, the violinist and attorney-to-be Julia Stahlkuppe, and the persistent book-loving Alexandra Stahlkuppe.

Acknowledgments

Many thanks go to Cesar Millan, Ken Foster, Jim Gorant, and Diane Jessup who have put their love for the American Pit Bull Terrier into words and actions. Pit Bull Rescue Central (PBRC) who have done so much in their contacts throughout North America to rescue pit bulls and similar dogs, deserve highest praise.

This handbook is dedicated to those people who have opened their homes and hearts to adopt APBTs in desperate need of a caring and safe environment.

I also want to thank Tiffany Riccio, Kevin Ryan, and the wonder-of-wonders of editors, Angela Tartaro, for those timeless efforts and limitless patience in helping me complete this revision. On the home front, my wife Cathie has been a wise ongoing source of encouragement and support.

Lastly, I would like to share this book with the American veterans, especially my fellow Vietnam co-warriors, who have undergone some of the same prejudiced public responses as have the American Pit Bull Terriers.

Photo Credits

123rf.com: Jim Boardman: page 61; Bonzami Emmanuelle: page 124; Jan de Wild: pages 10, 110; Jiri Hamhalter: page 14; Erik Lam: page 45; Ali Peterson: pages 26, 43, 70, 165; Anna Yakimova: page 64.

Modern Life Photo: page 34.

Seth Casteel: page 101.

PassionPetPhotos.com-Cheryl Carogan: pages 36, 175.

MaxDogPhoto.com: page 68.

jeanmfogle.com: pages 76, 87, 98, 103, 136, 172.

istock.com: Brian Asmussen: page 123; Jonathan Brizendine: pages 50, 73, 84, 92, 122; Jesse DeGraff: page 168; Alexandra Draghici: page 132; Arthur Carlo Franco: page 117; Melissa Meints: page 108; Ploughmann: page 156; Alex Potemkin: page 88; Cameron Whitman: pages 113, 140; Micah Young: page 118.

Oh My Dog! Photography: pages 6, 16, 22.

Paws on the Run: page 51.

Shutterstock.com: aerogondo2: page 129; Ilka Antonova: page 19; Best Shots: page 63; Lars Christensen: page 119; cynoclub: pages 100, 169; Dapixstudio: page 149; Jan de Wild: page 139; dogboxstudio: pages 4, 71, 78, 121, 166; elena: page 80; Espelt Photography: page 72; fotoedu: page 134; Billy Gadbury: page 62; Hamik: page 150; Eric Isselee: pages 3, 31, 32, 56, 66, 86, 90, 94, 120, 142, 163; kostudio: page 83; Erik Lam: pages 17, 25, 28, 38, 47, 55, 81; Sergey Lavrentev: pages 33, 58, 114; George Lee: page 127; Lenkadan: page 30; ots-photo: page 57; Ksenia Raikova: page 99; Julia Remezova: pages 9, 39; rthoma: page 79; Robynrg: page viii; Phillip Alexander Russell: page 13; Peggy Woods Ryan: page 48; steamroller_blues: pages 153, 160; Susan Schmitz: page 23; Kazlouski Siarhei: page 53; Colton Stiffler: page v; Andrew Williams: page 105.

Joan Hustace Walker: pages 5, 20, 69, 97, 106, 130, 141, 145, 146.

All inquiries should be addressed to:
Barron's Educational Series, Inc.
250 Wireless Boulevard
Hauppauge, New York 11788
www.barronseduc.com

ISBN: 978-0-7641-4744-9

Library of Congress Catalog Card No. 2012955611

Printed in China
9 8 7 6 5 4 3 2 1

Cover Photos

123rf.com: Erik Lam: back cover (bottom).

Seth Casteel: back cover (top).

istock.com: jbrizendine: front cover (top).

Shutterstock.com: Four Oaks: front cover (bottom); Eric Isselee: front cover (center); Sergey Lavrentev: spine; tsik: inside back cover; Vera Zinkova: inside front cover.

Contents

The APBT—
A New View

An APBT Scenario

The little girl, about four years old, was playing in the backyard of her suburban Florida home. She had carefully arranged her dolls for a tea party. Her mother was watching her out of the kitchen window. So intent was the child in her pretending that she sensed nothing amiss, no danger.

In this same suburb, two or three houses up the street, lived a powerful American Pit Bull Terrier. Seven years old, a muscular 45 pounds, he was covered with scars from his years as a fighting dog. Rescued from the pit, the dog lived his new life in comfort. At times, however, this pit veteran would escape from his backyard. Today was just such a time.

Jumping up on an outdoor grill, he cleared the backyard fence. As he walked down the street, he sensed movement from the little girl's backyard and headed in that direction. The child didn't see him enter her yard. She didn't see him fixate on her. She didn't see the intent look in his eyes. She didn't

see him when he started his charge toward her.

The child's mother saw the dog hurtling toward her daughter, but she didn't have time to call out. The little girl looked up and saw the rapidly approaching dog. She screamed as the animal leaped toward her. The dog jumped over the little girl and landed squarely atop a large rattlesnake coiled only a few feet away. Though severely bitten by the rattler, the dog easily killed the snake. He then vigorously shook the still-writhing body.

The child's mother ran to gather up her crying child and the dog dropped the snake and ran over to the little girl and began covering her face with licks of affection. When she arrived, the child's mother saw her daughter, the dog, and the twitching snake. She embraced the child and the dog, an old family friend.

Hype About APBTs

Perhaps you had envisioned a different ending to this short and true story. If you did, you may have been affected by the hype and fright-writing that has surrounded the American Pit Bull Terrier (APBT) over the past few decades. If the dog in this true scenario had been a Saint Bernard, a Beagle, or a Collie, would you have similar apprehensions about what was going to happen? Probably not. APBTs (and kindred breeds) have been the victims of more bad press, rumor, innuendo, myth, and fathomless fear than any dog breed in history.

For some reason it has been easier, certainly in past years, to believe the worst about the American Pit Bull Terrier. That was not always the case. For nearly a century, this breed was accepted as a valued family pet. True, he generally had to be watched around certain other kinds of dogs, but no more so than other large or powerful breeds. For ordinary Americans, especially in the tense times before World War I, the APBT epitomized the American spirit of strength and independence. Some time in the early-to-mid-1970s this public perception changed. An often wrongfully accused old family friend suddenly became Canine Public Enemy Number One.

This book is not about the "pit bull." This book is about the American Pit Bull Terrier. The two are *not* the same. "Pit bulls" can be almost anything. They can be poorly bred pit fighting dogs, poorly bred American Staffordshire Terriers, poorly bred Staffordshire Bull Terriers, poorly bred APBTs, mixed dogs of

some bull breed heritage, or just shorthaired and thickset mongrels with an attitude. This book is about a great and misunderstood American canine treasure, a breed of dog that has conquered more obstacles than any other breed of dog in the history of the human-canine relationship. It is about dogs that many consider the greatest all-around breed to ever exist, a breed with a long and distinguished history as one of the gentlest and most versatile of family pets, the bravest of war dogs, and the staunchest defenders of children. This book, without a hint of apology, is about the American Pit Bull Terrier.

The APBT as a Family Pet and Companion

The APBT is a dog of extremes. He is extremely strong, extremely powerful, and extremely loyal. He evokes extreme reactions, positive *and* negative. An alert and intelligent breed, the APBT has not only participated in, but has also excelled in, almost every activity in which dogs can be involved. In obedience, agility, therapy work, hunting, Schutzhund, weight-pulling contests, and candidly, in the dog-fighting pit, the APBT has continually surprised those who know the breed best and has amazed the uninitiated. However, this beautiful, powerful, bright, clownish, controversial dog has done his best work as a family pet and companion animal.

As serious students of canines, breed experts and anyone who has spent any length of time with a good APBT will readily testify that this breed, properly bred and properly socialized, is *the least likely of all breeds to bite a human being!* Many self-anointed guardians of all-things-canine may not accept this fact, but their ignorance does not make the fact less true. Historically, when they were pit fighting dogs, APBTs were bred never to attack humans. Their owners eliminated dogs that did not conform to this strict ideal.

Appearance

Size

There is some degree of diversity in appearance among American Pit Bull Terriers. APBTs can range in size from 30 pounds to 75 pounds (14 to 34 kg). Some breeders, as they have in so many other breeds, have even produced giant versions of the APBT, approaching 100 pounds (45 kg) or more. Some of the original pit fighting dogs imported from the British Isles were very small by today's standards. In the pit, some of the greatest fighters of all time weighed less than 35 pounds (16 kg). These dogs gave rise to the popular expression, "It is not the size of the dog in the fight; it's the size of the fight in the dog."

Color

The APBT can be any solid shade or combination of colors. Solid colors often show off the rippling muscles of the breed. Spotted or bicolored dogs are often quite attractive. Their white markings provide striking contrasts. Brindle (a red or tan dog overshot with black striping), fawn (in many tones), red, blue, or black APBTs can be beautiful. Solid white is allowed in the APBT, but not in the APBT's cousin-breed, the American Staffordshire Terrier (Amstaff).

Color really never played much of a role in the APBT. The imported Irish dogs of the late 1800s were often solid red or red with white markings. Perhaps the result of

closely bred lines, the early imported red dogs—especially with red noses—were often descendants of a well-known strain or family of pit dogs. Even today, when legendary pit dogs are discussed, the term, "Old-Family Red-Nose," usually comes up in the conversation. Several well-known modern American dog breeders have continued to propagate dogs of this color and of this bloodline or family.

What Your APBT Needs

The well-bred, well-socialized American Pit Bull Terrier can be an excellent family pet, but the APBT is not the dog for everyone. First-time dog owners would certainly be well advised to serve a lengthy apprenticeship with some other kind of dog before undertaking the challenge of owning an APBT, the Amstaff, or any of what is called the "bull breeds." An experienced dog person, intent on learning about the APBT, should have no difficulty owning a dog of this breed. Much like a spirited horse, the APBT requires a human owner that can handle such a dog, meet its needs, and avoid potential problems.

Socialization

Socialization (page 85) is crucial for any young dog, but absolutely essential for the APBT puppy. Smart dog owners know that a "no surprises" attitude is best when

owning dogs of any large and powerful breed. Everything that is true for these other breeds is even truer for the APBT.

Training

No other breed of dog needs the benefit of good training more than the APBT. For any breed with an aggressive heritage, ample training is an absolute must. If you don't want to take the time to see that your pet is thoroughly trained, or if training is an aspect of dog ownership that doesn't interest you, forget the APBT and find some other breed, or maybe just forego dog ownership altogether!

Traits

Loyalty and Fun

As a pet, the well-bred, well-socialized, and well-trained American Pit Bull Terrier is a great choice. Before "pit bull hysteria" started, stories about great APBTs were common. Thousands of APBTs lived long and happy lives. They are very loyal and there is absolutely no breed readier to give his life in protection of his family. They are also easy to groom. The breed is generally blessed with robust health. Seemingly built in to APBTs is an active love of life and, running counter to their public perception, an innate clownishness.

Aggressiveness

There are aspects of owning an APBT that require alert, aware, and

careful owners. For example, some APBTs may show aggression especially to other aggressive dogs. Since, pound for pound, the APBT is the strongest dog in the world, one must be prepared to prevent impromptu scuffles and other problems *before* they occur.

Most other breeds and breed types briefly tussle, then one or the other will submit to the more dominant and thus the conflict ends. This matter of dominance/submission does not work the same way with the pit dog breeds.

Most APBTs that are family pets never get into a serious fight, and many go through their entire lives without ever showing overt aggression to a nonthreatening dog. This is largely due to the fact that these APBTs have owners who understand them. To an APBT, and to similar dog breeds and types, fighting can be like alcohol is to an alcoholic or drugs to a drug addict. Temperance is always

great dog, take great care to find and develop one for yourself and your family. You'll be happy you did. Act impulsively and you will come to rue the day you ever thought about owning a dog.

The APBT Versus the "Pit Bull" Terror

A number of breeds have been forced to wear the unjust mantle of "canine Frankenstein." Great Danes, now one of the mildest of dogs, once wore it. Malamutes, German Shepherd Dogs, Dobermans, and Akitas have worn it. Wolf-dog hybrids, Rottweilers, and Chow Chows still sometimes wear it. But no breed of dog in history has ever been loaded down with as much terribly evil baggage as has the APBT.

Fans of the breed look back to the good old days when their dogs got positive, or at least neutral, grades in the minds of the general public. In the past two decades, the instant-information society caught up with and chronicled every dog bite and attack occurring anywhere in the civilized world. Tabloid journalists—and some writers and broadcasters who simply didn't dig deep enough—got the most exposure possible out of these incidents. Some sensationalized their accounts simply by affixing the "pit bull" tag. Bogus dog bite victims have found that their pleas for sympathy and

recommended, and abstinence is desired; wise dog owners will strive to keep their APBTs out of situations where fighting is a possibility.

Good Health

The American Pit Bull Terrier is an unusually healthy breed. The rigors of his pit dog history have not given way to the many hereditary diseases or physical conditions that plague so many other purebred dog breeds. Good basic veterinary care is usually enough to give the APBT a chance at a long and full life. Preventive care and accident avoidance should be all that is needed to keep such a pet healthy.

The APBT can be just right for those humans capable of understanding him and of providing the right training, care, and environment for this breed. No dog of any breed or mixture of breeds should be obtained on impulse and certainly not an APBT. If you want a possible legal claims are greatly strengthened if the incident in question involved the "dreaded pit bull."

Human-aggressive "Pit Bulls"

Throughout this book, the name American Pit Bull Terrier or APBT refers only to actual dogs that are of that specific breed. "Pit" or "pit bull" (used here only in lower-case letters) is used to indicate dogs of less certain heritage. Anyone can choose to call his or her dog anything. This misnaming has greatly contributed to the bad rap legitimate APBTs have received. When any medium-sized, short-haired mongrel is misidentified as a "pit bull" or as a "part-pit bull," that information may be the only thing that the listener or reader remembers.

Pit dogs could conceivably be of any breed. The irresponsible street pit fighters of today are constantly crossing, recrossing, and cross-crossing to gain some sort of perceived or imagined fighting advantage. Because the key ingredient in any pit dog must be gameness, this resorting to non-game breeds is foolish. Where, in years gone by, the APBTs of actual fighting strains were aggressive only toward other pit dogs, the mixed pit dogs of today are often aggressive toward dogs *and* humans. These dogs account for a vast proportion of the terrible dog bites and fatalities that so greatly contribute to the "pit bull terror" that seized the American psyche.

Certainly there have been horrible attacks by dogs said to be "pit bulls." Some of these, especially involving children, have indeed been gruesome and tragic. Strangely though, even as the reputation of these dogs headed into the cesspool of public opinion, the popularity of the "pit bull" in some elements of the community grew at a phenomenal rate. Most of these new pit people wanted vicious dogs for a variety of unwise, unsavory, and illegal reasons. They began to indiscriminately breed their dogs. Viciousness and aggressiveness became prized commodities in a new type of pit dog. Soon, human-aggressive APBT-type dogs became fairly common. Human-aggressive APBTs and similar dogs had been extremely rare until the1970s. Poorly bred, poorly socialized, and poorly trained animals suddenly grew into many thousands of these powerful and temperamentally unsound "pit bulls." These poor imitations of the true APBT are responsible for the vast majority of the actual dog bites and attacks blamed on this breed.

The Media

Some print and broadcast journalists saw the name "pit bull" as a way to insure a wider audience for their news stories. Rather than check out the actual kind of dog involved in a dog bite, or the circumstances under which these bites occurred, some newspeople were content to take the first version of an incident that they heard. Unfortunately, a class of "killer dogs" developed in the public mentality from their poor reporting. Suddenly, as if in a self-fulfilling prophecy, every dog bite became a "pit bull" attack. Boxers, yellow Labs, and all short-haired, medium-sized mongrels were transformed into "pit bulls" or the equally vague, "pit bull-mixes."

American Staffordshire Terriers, Staffordshire Bull Terriers, Bull Terriers, Boxers, Bull Mastiffs, and other breeds suffered right along with the APBT. The public believed what they heard or read about this new canine scourge, a sort of Attila the Hound. A *War of the Worlds* mentality took over as headlines on the evening news read: "Two pit bulls terrorize small town" or "Policeman savaged by pit bull." Combined with all the false "pit bull" stories or accusations were legitimate accounts that did actually involve some APBTs, Amstaffs, Staffy Bulls, and others. Unable and perhaps unwilling to put the "pit bull" genie back into the bottle, a media avalanche swept away the nearly 100 years of good reputation that the American Pit Bull Terrier had earned.

Branding Owners

People, who weren't dog-friendly even before the hype began, started to speak out against these fearsome creatures that were a plague to all decent people. Law enforcement spokespersons told about the use of the "pit bulls" by drug dealers and other criminals to intimidate citizens and guard clandestine drug labs and marijuana patches. If you happened to own an APBT, or a dog that even remotely resembled an APBT, you were often branded at the worst, demonic, and at the best, crudely eccentric. If you owned two such dogs or happened to have a litter of APBT puppies, some labeled you as the kingpin of a dog-fighting ring located in your garage, basement, or guest room. Occasionally, operating on an anonymous tip, vice cops and animal cruelty officers would raid a household suspected of being a haven for pit bulls, only to discover an aging Boston Terrier or an arthritic Pug as the only dog living in the home.

Criminals and Gangs

This hysteria strangely had an added bonus for the people who so greatly caused it—drug dealers, gang members, and other street criminals. They gained immeasurably in terms of added reputation and intimidation potential when their pit-type dogs instilled fear in the general communities. These thugs often created situations in which the savagery of their dogs could be prominently displayed.

Owning the most feared dog on the block became a goal. These street punks-turned-dogfighters were far removed from the pit dog-fighters of the earlier part of this century. This new dog-fighting element quickly outraged the American people in a way the traditional fighters never had. Accounts of renewed fights and actual crimes using "pit bulls" as weapons were duly reported, and the dog breed with the wrong name at the wrong time—the APBT—gained a completely undeserved reputation as a canine monster. This myth grew and grew.

Some communities have piously tried to sweep their streets of the effects of the drug dealers and criminals. In a time of enlightened civic responsibility, these cities banned the dogs they most closely identified with the punks and criminals. Since the leaders of some cities were content to remain in a state of ignorance in response to a public outcry, they banned *all* APBTs and certain judiciously selected other breeds.

Rediscovering This Breed

People are often interested in new breeds, exotic breeds, breeds from long ago or far away. One excellent way to gain a new look at any breed is to approach such a breed as if it had just surfaced. Breeds such as the Dogo de Argentino, the Akita, the Tosa Inu, the Anatolian Shepherd, and others are large, sometimes quite aggressive dogs. Unfortunately, the supporters of these dogs often fail to mention (or perhaps consider) aggressiveness or problem potential. These breeds have been heralded as "new" even though some of them are actually very ancient in heritage.

Each is much larger than the APBT and could inflict substantial injury to humans or to other dogs. Interestingly, these large and aggressive "new" breeds don't yet face the prejudice confronting the American Pit Bull Terrier.

Let us observe the APBT as if we had never heard of or seen the breed before. This breed may look quite different if we view it without any preconceived attitudes and we would probably herald it as the next wonder dog. There are many reasons that this "new" breed would gain immediate positive acceptance:
• It has a medium-length, low-maintenance coat, and is remarkably hardy.
• It is athletic, capable of many versatile roles and activities.
• It has an eye-catching, sturdy frame, available in many color and size variations.

- It has a long and distinguished record as a movie star, as a war dog, and as a therapy dog.
- It is active enough for the grandchildren, yet reserved enough for the grandparents.

There are many more attributes of this breed that could be added to the list. A simple truth exists: If the APBT was to suddenly come onto the canine scene, he would be widely accepted and would be acclaimed as the next great dog breed. Instead of Jack Russell Terriers, which are very similar to APBTs in temperament, on sitcoms and in commercials, theatrical agents, film producers, and maddening crowds of fans would besiege APBTs. Any minor indiscretions that a particular APBT might commit would be considered all part of the unique character of this wonderful "newly discovered" breed.

APBTs and Other Dogs

Failing to offset all the good qualities of this "new" breed would be one negative element, which has been present in the newfound breeds such as the highly popular Jack Russell Terrier and the Chinese Shar-pei. This element is a definite level of aggressiveness by some members of the breed toward other dogs. Almost every purebred or mixed-breed dog can show this same tendency, if poorly socialized. In the "new breed" scenario, dog experts would quickly rush to the APBT's defense stating that it is highly probable that ordinary good judgment and everyday preventive

- It is highly intelligent and very trainable, an obedience/agility/Schutzhund candidate.
- It is courageous and protective.
- It is excellent with adults and children.
- It is loyal, with lots of personality, and often quite clownish.
- Its ears can be cropped or left natural; the visual effect is much the same either way.
- It is not prone to many inheritable health problems or conditions.
- It is an excellent companion and pet.
- It is a good traveler, easily adaptable to most lifestyles and living arrangements.
- It has a strikingly forceful, yet attractive appearance, a definite crime deterrent.
- It is physically tough, with some hunting dog potential.

measures would greatly calm any apprehension about aggressiveness in the "newly discovered" APBT.

Legal Lightning Rod

With the development of a widely accepted public perception of the APBT as the "Bogey-Dog" came the first of a group of legal remedies designed to protect society from the canine equivalent to the great white shark. First came restrictions on all breeds, some of which were reasonable, such as leash laws and dog licensing. The day of the household pet unrestrictedly roaming the community was over, and rightfully so. Again, this was a positive move that effectively brought to an end much of the mischief unattended dogs can get into. It also helped lower the number of dog deaths caused by cars and trucks. Dog bites went down. Altercations between dogs went down. Unwanted litters dropped.

Many people began walking with their dogs, jogging with their dogs, promenading with their dogs on city streets, in city parks, and along suburban avenues. A new type of conflict began to result from this new activity. Some people couldn't (or wouldn't) control their pets. Others actually seemed to enjoy strutting through the community with a large, impressive, possibly aggressive, dog. The element of human ineptitude and ego actually produced a worse situation than had existed in some communities *before* leash laws and other restraints took effect.

In the pre-leash law days, free-ranging dogs in a particular area often came to mutual understandings among themselves about who was the strongest and meanest dog. Most spur-of-the-moment dogfights ended with one dog submitting to another. The loser would find a different fire hydrant and a different place in the pecking order. This peace would last until some new challenger arrived to change the balance of power. These informal rank orderings, structured by the canines themselves, disappeared when dogs were kept behind fences. The human element entered the equation.

In most communities there were usually restrained animals, even before leash laws. Many APBT owners, and owners of similar dogs, kept their animals securely behind fences. The APBT was not, and is not now, a dog to be allowed in the informal community leadership ladder contests. The APBT owner knew that and few problems occurred. Owners of other dogs allowed their dogs to run free, but the wise APBT owner never would take this chance.

When unwise and impulsive people began to see that the "pit bull" could be an effective tool in fostering a tough image, the breed began its downhill slide. Dogs of the "pit" type began to be bred not for their usual companionable traits, but for aggressiveness, first toward the other guy's dog, then toward the other guy.

"Pit bulls" that would have, in earlier times, been destroyed by their owners as temperamentally unsound, suddenly became highly sought after as breeding stock. Mean and vicious dogs were mated with mean and vicious dogs and the meanest and most vicious pups prized as future breeders. Then supply and demand with the "puppy mill effect" took over and an ample supply of bad dogs was built up to meet the great demand for them. Uncertain temperament, long banned from even dogfight pits, suddenly became a selling point for a street pit stud dog or brood bitch.

The APBT may have, in some very extended way, been the starting point for this degradation of a breed, but soon the dogs being produced by this segment of the population weren't APBTs anymore. These canine misfits became a new type of dog altogether, but the little three-letter-word "pit" stuck and became the only real connection between thug-owned street pits and the true APBT.

To make matters worse, the same dangerous breeding practices were going on in other large breeds. Dogs that were significantly larger than the APBT were bred to the same aggressive standards, and then these larger dogs were crossed with the "pit bulls." These intermingling of pit and other large and aggressive breeds produced large and powerful and quite vicious dogs that did share some pit dog genetic heritage. These new canine powder kegs were also often simply called "pit bulls."

Just as some poorly bred APBTs may have produced some of the vicious street pit dogs, thugs often spawn would-be thugs in the general population. Insecure and impressionable "camp followers" often identified with roguish street toughs and their "pit" dogs. While not necessarily gang members or even criminals themselves, these impressionable neophytes emulated the bad dudes with the bad attitudes and the bad dogs. No longer were the trappings of thugdom relegated to the inner-city or to unsafe streets. Misplaced hero worship brought this developing nightmare right onto the suburban streets of middle class America.

The average working person, the older pensioner, the student, and the innocent child began to come into contact with "pit bulls," those sad and increasingly more dangerous representatives of the canine world. Bites and attacks naturally ensued and the media picked up on the "pit bulls."

Laws

Laws targeting these dogs (see Breed-specific Legislation, page 74) became a shotgun solution to the blight caused by the invasion of these dogs. When the citizens groups, city councils, and legislatures sought to identify the culprits, guilt by supposed association took over. The "pit bulls" that the laws and regulations sought to banish became the APBTs, the Staffordshire Bull Terriers, the Bull Terriers, the American Staffordshire Terriers, and other pure breeds. The laws may have been just and well intentioned, but the targets were the wrong dogs.

We have also become a litigious society. Lawsuits and legal actions began to center on any area of real or imagined personal injury. The emerging "pit bull" became a litigator's dream. An unsavory dog with a bad reputation owned by a real or imitation criminal type wouldn't find many friends among the judiciary or among juries. Certainly, some dog bite cases were horrendous. Small children killed or frightfully maimed should make every reasonable person shudder. Dog bites, especially by large and powerful dogs, can be crippling and disfiguring. Legal remedies and public outrage in such cases are certainly more than appropriate, but unfortunately, society tends to use a broad brush in inflicting our retribution.

The APBT by Any Other Name

The "pit bull" epithet given to any dogs that even remotely fit this image has resulted in a great deal of carnage among innocent dogs. Either the word "pit" or the word "bull" came to generate public indignation. Even the squat and humorous Bulldog (known colloquially as the *English* Bulldog) has not escaped some heat.

Many breeds and mixes have become victims of mistaken identity. In the quest to rid the world from the vicious and hyperaggressive street pits, well-intentioned, but ignorant souls have caused many of these other dogs to be given the mark of a canine Cain. That the vast proportion of the dogs in these breeds are excellent pets hasn't stopped people from seeking out and eliminating any vestige of a dog that might just be a "pit bull."

The APBT receives most of the grief. This breed has the misfortune to have both "pit" and "bull" in its name. This breed also provided some of the genetic material that went to make the street pits that have been the actual cause of much pain, anguish, and misunderstanding. The APBT is also a dog that needs reasonable precautions when it confronts other dogs, but the APBT and these other breeds mentioned earlier are no more dangerous to people than any other breed and considerably less than some.

The APBT suffers because of look-alike and sound-alike dogs that do bad things.

Chapter Two

History and Heritage of the APBT

The APBT is not American in lineage, and it has not always been called by this name. Some other terrier breeds considered the word "bull" as their private property. Some others argued that the breed is not even a terrier and really should be called a "bulldog." One of the largest dog registries in the world could not abide the word "pit" in the breed's name, so they renamed the breed and accepted their creation into membership

The history and heritage of the APBT spans most of this millennium. The excellent APBT of today is descended from some of the most powerful canines ever known. To begin to understand this breed, it is necessary to start with some of the key elements that were brought together, honed in battle and bloodshed, refocused, and then shaped into the American Pit Bull Terrier.

Mastiffs and Bulldogs

One of the oldest of all dog classifications is the widely diverse and extended breed group of the mastiff (or mollossus) family.

Note: For this book, breed names will be capitalized; breed types (and general groupings) will not.

Most typically, the mastiff breeds are giants, tall and heavy. They have been spread around the world and many countries have their own mastiff breed. Large bones, great height, great weight, and often very large heads and clearly defined features are points of identification for the mastiff breeds.

The mastiff family includes both well-known and lesser-known breeds;

• The Mastiff, sometimes referred to as the *English Mastiff*, a huge fawn or brindle giant, was the favorite of kings and commoners in England. The Mastiff is recognized as near kin to the other giants in the family that bears its name.

• The Great Dane, called the *German Mastiff* in much of Europe, is taller and slimmer, but clearly still a mastiff. Irish Wolfhounds, and perhaps Greyhounds helped give this tall breed a powerful, but less bulky appearance.

• The Dogue de Bordeaux, or *French Mastiff*, was popularized in the United States to some extent, by the Tom Hanks' film, *Turner and Hooch*. Not quite as large as the Mastiff of England, the Dogue de Bordeaux has a huge head and is recognized in only a reddish fawn with a muzzle that can be red or black.

• The Saint Bernard, or *Alpine Mastiff*, is known worldwide for its reputation as a finder of avalanche victims and other lost souls attempting to cross the Saint Bernard Pass in the Swiss Alps. Though the brandy keg on his collar probably is a myth, the Saint comes in two coat lengths, rough and smooth.

• The Newfoundland is water safety's equivalent to the snow-oriented Saint Bernard. Newfies are legendary for

saving drowning people. Quite large and mastiff-like, Newfoundlands—named after the Canadian region of Newfoundland—have long coats and are solid black, brown (bronze), or gray, and also *Landseer*, which is black and white. In some countries the Landseer is recognized as a separate breed.

• The Bullmastiff is a member of both the mastiff and bulldog families, resulting from a cross between the large bulldog of England, not the short modern dog with the smashed-in face, and the Mastiff. Originally meant to make the giant Mastiff quicker and more agile, the Bullmastiff, as an estate gamekeeper's dog, became the poacher's worst nightmare.

• The Rottweiler is another mastiff breed of German extraction. The Rott was originally a cattle dog, but has become the most popular mastiff breed in the United States.

• The Pug is both the only Chinese member of the mastiff group, and the smallest mastiff. The Pug is really a mastiff in miniature and comes in fawn (apricot) and black.

• The Bulldog, once called the *English Bulldog*, actually has a family of breeds of its own, but is also clearly descended from the mastiffs. Today's Bulldog is more of a pet and canine curiosity than the other much larger and more rugged mastiff family members.

• The Staffordshire Bull Terrier is the British version of the fighting pit terrier. As with the Bulldog, the Staffordshire Bull Terrier has been greatly bred away from any of its original purposes, with the modern dogs being short, squat, and more pet dog than pit dog.

• The American Staffordshire Terrier and the APBT were the same dogs until the mid-1930s when the "pit" part of the United Kennel Club's (UKC) name for the breed found hostility at the AKC. The AKC, at a loss for a name, accepted "Staffordshire Terrier" in its attempt at refurbishing the APBT. Later, in the 1970s, the additional name "American" Staffordshire Terrier had to be added to avoid confusion with the new AKC member from England, the Staffordshire Bull Terrier. Having been bred for conformation for over half a century, the Amstaff is now primarily prized more for his looks than for his working abilities.

• The APBT is the American version of the pit fighting dog that remained with his more appropriate name after the Amstaff was developed and moved on to the AKC. The APBT is one of the most popular dogs worldwide.

• The Bull Terrier (white and colored) is another English product. Handsome in its long-faced, "Spuds McKenzie" way, the Bull Terrier was called a fighter. Revisionist history to the contrary, the Bull Terrier was never really much of a fighting dog and was developed by James Hinks of Birmingham (England) in the 1860s. Hinks, using Spanish Pointer, pit dog (Staffordshire Bull Terrier), and Dalmatian bloodlines, created an elegant show dog that looked like it might have been able to fight.

• The Tibetan Mastiff is possibly the oldest of the mastiff family and is suspected to be the genetic source from which the other mastiffs descended. A medium-large longhaired dog, the Tibetan Mastiff was featured in the film, *Man's Best Friend*.

• The Tosa Inu is a giant fighting mastiff from Japan. Through much ceremony, this "Sumo pit bull" battles other Tosas in Japan, where such activities are still legal. Much larger than the APBT, the Tosa has also been outlawed in Britain and a number of other places.

• The Dogo Argentino is a large Argentine import that looks like a giant, solid white APBT, even down to the cropped ears. The Dogo, the only dog breed developed in Argentina, was originally bred (from several European breeds) to hunt cougars, jaguars, and wild boars.

- The Fila Brasileiro is a Brazilian mastiff with a considerable amount of Bloodhound and Mastiff in his genetic makeup. The Fila was originally a hunting dog that was used occasionally to track runaway slaves and criminals. They are now used to help with the semiwild Brazilian cattle and have become popular in the United States.
- The Neapolitan Mastiff is an Italian giant that may trace directly back to the mastiffs that fought in the Roman arenas. Neos are slate gray, black, mahogany, and blond. Their ears are sometimes cut quite short, which lends to the breed's ferocious appearance.
- The American Bulldog is not at all like the Bulldog (of English origin). Resembling more a Bullmastiff, the American Bulldog is a strong dog that is often used in weight-pulling events. A product of the United States, this breed is fast gaining approval as a family protection dog.
- Other members of the mastiff family, and the extended family that includes descendants of the mastiff through the bulldogs, are: Boston Terriers, French Bulldogs, and Boxers.

Most of the giant breeds and many of the working breeds stem directly from the early mastiff-type dogs. Thought to be of Tibetan origins, the mastiff breeds found their way over much of the globe. Their impressive size was sometimes exaggerated a bit, but their valor as war dogs and personal protection dogs gave the mastiffs a value in the world of kings, armies, and arenas.

Fighting Canines

Many of the early mastiffs found their way into the arenas in far-flung corners of the Roman Empire. Fighting every kind of creature from man to lions, and even elephants, mastiffs became the epitome of savagery and fighting ability. Because these traits were highly valued in barbaric civilizations, these dogs were greatly prized and became gifts for visiting kings and noblemen. The gift of these animals to the leaders of other countries helped in the spread of mastiff genetic material.

Mastiffs were truly awesome fighting machines. Their huge size was amply complemented by vicious and savage dispositions. To augment the dogs' natural abilities as fighters, they were often outfitted with bladed collars and armor. Used in much the same way that sappers or shock troops would be used in later warfare, these fighting dogs served both as vanguard attack forces and as diversionary tactical elements. While opposing foot soldiers were occupied battling the giant dogs, the dogs' masters would swoop down in a cavalry charge. If the mounted battlers went in first, the mastiffs were restrained and set free at the right moment to turn the tide of a skirmish or battle.

The mastiff forces fought in many wars over many centuries. Art on ancient tombs clearly reflects an identifiable mastiff-type dog attacking mounted riders. Mastiffs were even used in the conquest of the New World when they were set on native tribes with devastating effect. Kings kept great kennels of these fierce war dogs. One Egyptian pharaoh had a retinue of over 2,000 canine fighters in his army. These impressive weapons did not go unnoticed by the conquering Romans who soon added these dogs to their forces.

Rome was successful enough at war to have sufficient disposable time and funds to bring back some of the horrors of war to the home folks. Arenas found the mastiff fighting again, and against all manner of creatures. These early dogs, often blendings of several types of mastiffs the Romans had encountered in their conquests, were often left behind in the countries that had become part of the Roman Empire. They were bred to local dogs, and many new breeds resulted. Over 40 modern breeds can directly be traced to mastiff ancestry. All of these breeds except four, the Boston Terrier, the Pug, the French Bulldog, and the Miniature Bull Terrier, are still reminiscent of the power and strength of their Mollosian forebears—the mastiffs.

The Middle Ages: During the Middle Ages, cannons and other devices of destruction were surpassed in the killing and maiming power of the mastiff regiments. These giant and still quite aggressive dogs became manor dogs guarding nobility. The big dogs became hunters to battle wolves, bears, and other marauders. They still belonged largely to the feudal lords. In England and throughout Europe giant mastiff

dogs began to fill a function quite similar to that of their ancestors in the Roman arenas. Mastiffs began to be matched against beasts, first as an economic necessity, then as a mini-spectacle, and then as a full-blown "sport."

Bullbaiting

Fierce mastiff dogs had long bedeviled bulls and bears. Germany had its *bullenbeisser* (bull biter) and *barenbeisser* (bear biter). Originally hunting mastiffs, these "biters" suddenly joined their distant relatives all over Europe in a new blood sport— the baiting of bulls and bears. As bears became rarer and harder to obtain, more and more attention was paid to battling bulls. Arenas were no longer available, but every village and town had its butcher shop/slaughterhouse. Bulls were baited—chained and then attacked by one or more dogs—in the town square and in any open areas where a crowd might easily view the spectacle.

Large, heavy-bodied mastiffs had plenty of courage, but their lack of quick and agile mobility caused many giant dogs to die in the bull-to-dog encounters. Quicker dogs, more successful in surviving these encounters, soon began to dominate the gene pool of bullbaiting dogs. In other countries, quicker dogs also began to replace the larger, slower mastiffs in battling bulls and the occasional bear.

The emergence of these quicker, lighter, and more agile dogs brought a resurgence of interest in bullbaiting contests. These improved new dogs were called by what they did, the canines were called "bulldogs," and they gradually replaced the mastiff breeds in several countries. The regions that had once boasted of their local mastiffs soon were touting the abilities of their local bulldogs. The bulldogs would prove to be more adaptable and more entertaining than their predecessors and achieved great popularity. Merchants and other travelers, much like the Romans had done with the mastiffs, soon spread bulldogs throughout the world.

Brabanters

In Germany, a smaller, shorter-limbed *bullenbeisser* began to be bred in the city of Brabant. These dogs were called Brabanters. A painting of this divergent bulldog-type done by John E. L. Riedinger of Augsberg around 1740 shows a well-muscled, medium-sized dog that looks much like the early bulldogs of England that, in turn, looks

distinctly like the APBTs of today. Research into the Brabanter found that this breed possessed many of the attributes admired in the early bulldogs and later in the APBT. Gameness (a primary APBT quality), the ability to stubbornly hang onto a bull, adaptability in working bulls or even swine, and sturdy, squarely built bodies were all well-known Brabanter characteristics.

The astute canine student and writer John P. "Jack" Wagner wrote in 1939 that the Brabanters (the small *bullenbeisser*) rather than the severely short-faced, undershot, and squatty English Bulldog were the probable ancestors of the Boxer. The Brabanter, to Wagner and several other experts, bore a remarkable resemblance to the APBT of today. Wagner even hypothesizes that the Bulldog could trace its genetic steps back to the mastiff through the smaller *bullenbeisser*, the Brabanter. Thus, this pocket version of the mastiff, the Brabanter, could possibly be the parent of the bulldogs that were later bred to be the Bulldog we know today. If this is true, the APBT could definitely descend from the Brabanter and similar tough, smaller mastiffs.

Many avowed modern game-bred—the term "game-bred" today is taken to mean dogs bred for fighting or other hunting sports—APBT breeders discount the "T" in APBT. They have long claimed that the APBT of today is not a mixture of terrier and bulldog as is commonly accepted as fact, but the lineal descendant of the actual early bull-dog. Wagner seemed to hold a similar view and his thinking centered on the Boxer, one of the bull breeds related to the APBT. Except for the head, the Boxer is a very similar breed in size and appearance to the APBT.

Terriers (Theoretically)

Some of the world's greatest terrier breeds come from England. With all due consideration to the bulldog-only claims of the game-bred APBT fans, it seems almost certain that the breed we know as the APBT is most assuredly of bulldog-and-terrier blending. The very availability of many excellent terriers in Britain bodes well for the proposition that these sturdy "earth dogs" fit in somewhere in the genetic amalgam that is the APBT.

That the word "terrier" has always been more or less historically attached to the pit dogs is another dispute to the "pure bulldog of ancient origins" theory held by many game-bred dog and dog-fighting enthusiasts. Even if the "bulldog" meant any dog that fought bulls, as some of this theory's proponents strongly assert, that does not mean that all dogs that later fought in the pit were *bulldogs*. This is more than just an argument based on semantics; this is an argument based on genetics.

Breeders of Germany's bulldog breed, the Boxer, have never denied that a Bulldog, Dr. Toenniessen's Tom (an English import) was the grandsire of the great matriarch of the Boxer breed, Meta Von der Passage No. 30. Meta appears in the extended pedigree of most of the great modern Boxers. Tom, the Bulldog, was described as not at all like the "… cloddy, low-to-the-ground, grotesque English Bulldog…"

Tom, also possibly contributed some of the genes for all-white and predominantly white dogs that still occasionally appear in Boxer litters to this day. Tom was "… muscular, square-built, long-legged," a small mastiff-type dog. Wagner says of Dr. Toenniessen's Tom, "He probably did much to help in those early days [1890s], particularly in speeding the arrival of our present head characteristics, which are so essential to good general appearance."

The point of mentioning the Boxer in the history of the APBT is that Boxer breeders strongly assert that their breed too has absolutely *no* terrier ancestry. None! The head of the Boxer is much more like that of a lightly built Bulldog than is the classic head of an APBT. If this one Bulldog, Dr. Toenniessen's Tom, impacted on the Boxer's head shape so much,

why then, if they are completely descended from the original bulldog of England, do not more APBTs have heads like Boxers? Could it be that APBTs have some terrier ancestry and Boxers don't? The long-held terrier theory makes as much sense as claiming that a breed that has been bred specifically for gameness and pit abilities would never have been crossed with terriers at any time over the past two centuries!

The pit dogs that became the ancestors of the APBT weren't the only pit fighting dogs in England, even if they were direct descendents of some sort of "original bulldog." In the *American Book of the Dog*, by Shields, 1891, an Englishman relates his story about his experienced fighting terrier "Crack," that killed his pit opponent in 48 minutes. He also had a bitch named "Floss." Floss fought a female pit dog (described as a bull-and-terrier) until "Floss set to and killed her." The defeated dogs were recognized pit dogs of the day while Crack and Floss were both Airedale Terriers.

This was a time when pit winners brought good prices and were bred to other pit winners to produce more pit winners. Is it really logical to believe that with dogs like Floss and Crack (and many other good fighting terriers), no significant terrier ancestry crept into the APBT?

British Attitudes of the Time

It is easy to sit in twenty-first century America and look back on the seventeenth century English and caustically criticize them for the wide variety of "blood sports" that were in evidence in that time. Without offering any defense for these bloody spectacles, an historical overview of the time may shed some light on why they did what they did. Perhaps this overview can also give some glimpse into the society that produced the bulldogs that fought bulls and bears (and other animals) and that provided the genetic framework, with or without the help of terriers, of the ancestors of the APBT.

Any student of English history during this period knows that life in the British Isles was quite harsh for the majority of the people. This majority excluded those of royalty, nobility, and wealth. Average Britons were abysmally poor. They could not read. They worked from dawn to past dusk at backbreaking work in mines, on small landholdings, at the docks, in factories, and as servants to the large landowners. Their lives were hard and short. In Ireland and Scotland, existence was even more precarious. Opportunities for pleasure and relief from drudgery were rare.

Perhaps as an opiate to their lives of pain and bleakness, the British developed a callused view of life. Cockfighting was brought to its highest zenith in the British Isles. Bull-

and bearbaiting were the only major diversions many common people had in their entire lives. When these activities were outlawed in 1835, they continued to be held clandestinely. But bears and bulls cannot be baited quietly in some out-of-the-way place. More often, a simpler form of blood sport, dogfighting, replaced bull- and bearbaiting. The British people's hard and brutal lives were sometimes reflected in the hardness and the brutality of the only spectator events they were able to see.

In bullbaiting and later, in dogfighting, the element of chance was always there. The much smaller dog might somehow triumph over the much larger bull or bear, just as a poor person might somehow one

A Tale of Two Terriers

A brother breed to the APBT is the Boston Terrier (colloquially and unpopularly still called the "Boston Bull Terrier" by uninformed people). The *original* Boston Terrier is clearly a very close relative of the original APBT. A number of books about the Boston Terrier make the following assertions:

• Both breeds were originally about the same size, approximately 35 pounds (16 kg).

• Hooper's "Judge," the founding sire of the Boston Terrier breed, was identified as a bull-and-terrier cross and was imported around 1865 from England by William O'Brien of Boston, Massachusetts.

• Judge, described as "more like a bulldog than a terrier" was dark brindle with white markings on his face and a white chest.

• Judge had cropped ears, a common surgery performed on pit dogs.

• Judge weighed 32 pounds (14.5 kg) and "...was a well-built and high stationed (tall) dog."

• Both breeds clearly demonstrated their bull-and-terrier heritage.

• An early name for the Boston was the "Round-headed Bull and Terrier."

• Another early name for the Boston was also an early name for the APBT, the "American Bull Terrier."

• Both breeds are athletic and packed with power; prominent writers still remark on how much the physiques of the two breeds look alike.

• Both were originally bred and then imported to America for the same purpose—to fight in the dog pits against other dogs.

• From bull-and-terrier stock, imported to the United States from Britain, the APBT was sent to fight in the pits.

• From bull-and-terrier stock, imported to the United States from Britain, the Boston Terrier was number one on the American Kennel Club's list of most popular breeds in America for many years.

day become a person of wealth. In dogfighting, a poor dogfighter who could develop a great dog could go head to head vicariously with the son of an earl or with the rich landed gentry. Just this glimmer of hope was enough for many poor Britons.

It would be unfair to the people of the United Kingdom to say that dog-fighting was universally accepted. It was not. Most of the population, rich and poor, felt the sport was cruel and that the practitioners were of a lower moral status, if not lower social status.

Many British residents felt they had a chance for a better life in America and immigrated to the

United States and Canada. They brought with them many of their customs, their language, their laws, and their blood sports.

Early Bulldogs

The bulldogs of the bull- and bear-baiting days were nothing like the snuffling, short-faced Bulldogs seen at the dog shows today. Bulldogs can be excellent pets, but their grotesque heads, bodies, and breathing apparatus prevent the kind of exertion required to tangle with an angry bear or bull or even an angry dog. The bulldogs of those early years about two-and-a-half centuries ago were quite different. In fact, the paintings of bulldogs of that time show them to closely resemble the APBTs and Amstaffs of our time.

Just as lighter, quicker, more agile dogs, such as Brabanter and the early bulldog, replaced the mastiffs in bull- and bearbaiting, so would a more nimble dog replace the bulldog as the primary fighting dog. This dog would need the bravery of the bulldog and the key ingredient, gameness, to become the preeminent pit dog.

Other Bull-and-Terrier Breeds

There are perhaps as many as 25 breeds, which stem from either the early bulldog or the bull-and-terrier crosses. These breeds include the APBT, the American Staffordshire Terrier, the Staffordshire Bull Terrier, the modern Bulldog, the French Bulldog, the Pug, the Boston Terrier, the Boxer, the Dogue de Bordeaux, the Bullmastiff, the Bull Terrier, the American Bulldog, and others.

Some of these breeds greatly resemble the APBT; others do not. When the resemblance is there, it is usually on a larger dog. Though the most accomplished fighting dog breed in the world, some countries thought that the APBT was too small and produced their own larger versions.

Chapter Three

The APBT: Coming to America

Legacies from England

A long with so many other things, the British brought with them their dogs when they arrived at the colonies in North America. Foxhounds, bird dogs, retrievers, and the ancestors of the APBT all made the voyage from the British Isles. These early fighting dogs were of the early bulldog and bull-and-terrier varieties. They were the same dogs that would supply the genetic stock for the APBT, the Amstaff, the Staffordshire Bull Terrier, and part of the heritage for the long-faced Bull Terrier.

These bulldogs and bull-and-terriers were welcomed in colonial America. As in Britain, the common people in America sought whatever diversions they could. Bullbaiting and later dogfighting filled much the same void for some Americans that it did for some of the British. Horse racing, cockfighting, bare-knuckle boxing, fox hunting, fly fishing, golf, game bird hunting with dogs, and other activities were all British imports. Fighting-dog breeders in the British

Isles found in America a ready market for any and all dogs they wanted to sell.

Bull- and bearbaiting, dog- and cockfighting were seen as ways to escape from the tedium of colonial life. Indian attacks, disease, disabling accidents, and urban and rural drudgery screamed for a release, if only momentarily, from hard and uncertain lives. In lives liberally laced with hardship, anxiety, and a struggle just to survive, the pit dog took on mythic proportions. The perils and tumult of the dog pit gave people an activity that, in some respects, mirrored their own lives.

The APBT in Early America

America was a still largely an untamed land and would remain so for many decades to come. Marauding Indian tribes, attacks by wild animals and general outlawry made frontier life less than safe. It not only created a climate for violent blood sports, but also bred a need for dogs

for protection, guarding, and hunting. Benjamin Franklin once proposed the importation of Mastiffs from England to serve as deterrents to Indian attacks in many frontier areas.

As civilization and industrialization spread from the East Coast westward, hard men in hard jobs kept to many of the same recreations as their British counterparts; among them drinking, fighting, gambling, and pit dog matches. Over a century of importation of fighting dogs from Britain produced pit dogs on a par with anything available across the water.

Following much the same path that Britain had taken, blood sports came onto the American continent and into the American psyche, flourished here, were outlawed, and still flourished. Meshing well with the myriad of other rough activities that characterize a frontier society, fights between dogs and other animals were both obvious and likely. Unlike Britain, the very scope of the American geography provided for greater regionalization. Something banned in the older cities and towns of New

England might continue with impunity half a continent away.

The Frontier

The pit dogs in frontier America were much more than just fighters for the pit. Many ancestors of the APBT were family and farm dogs. They regularly protected their owners' homesteads against predators, animal and human. They worked cattle. They served as hog catchers, which gave them the title of "catch dogs." They fought with wolves and coyotes, bears, and cougars, and sometimes on Saturdays, they fought against other pit dogs. Good stock dogs were valuable. Good hunting dogs were valuable. Good guard and watchdogs were valuable. Since many of these jobs were ably filled by the versatile APBT, these dogs were valuable, and since a good farm or frontier dog was a possible producer of other good dogs, early pit dogs also became ancestors for some of the better breeds ever to be produced in the United States. Many of these 100-year-old breeds that have been systematically ignored by some members of the show dog hierarchy have varying amounts of APBT in their genetic heritage.

The Curs: The Curs make up a group of versatile farm and hunting dog breeds. Their name, which is not meant in a disparaging way, may come from the practice of cutting off the puppies' tails or "cur-tailing" them. The Mountain Cur and the

Black Mouth Cur both somewhat resemble the APBT and they have some of the same qualities. They are among the original "can-do" dogs of the frontier farmstead. Curs are said to be loyal, even giving their lives for their families, which certainly sounds like an APBT trait.

The "Everydog"

Famous APBTs

The APBT, as the United States grew up, became a steady breed that was liked and respected by most of the population that came to know it. It became sort of an "Everydog" that embodied many of the things that Americans liked about their country and about themselves. The APBT was gradually thought of less as a pit fighter than as a regular dog with many admirable qualities; "Tige," the companion of "Buster Brown" of shoe fame was an APBT. By World War I the APBT had become an American symbol of reserved though tough neutrality, a canine version of the "Don't Tread on Me!" snake. Ironically, the APBT that served as the "neutrality with teeth" image before World War I was to become even more impressive in the form of "Stubby" the most decorated war dog of that war. Stubby was an APBT.

People had admiration and respect rather than fear of this former pit dog turned family dog. Helen Keller owned an APBT, as did heavyweight champ Jack Johnson.

President Theodore Roosevelt owned an APBT when he lived in the White House. Acknowledged worldwide as a great outdoorsman, Theodore Roosevelt was also an avid admirer of the APBT. In a January 18, 1901, letter to his daughter Ethel, from a western ranch, the robust President clearly states his feelings about the breed:

Darling Little Ethel,

I have had great fun. Most of the trip neither you nor Mother nor sister would enjoy, but you would all of you be immensely amused with the dogs. There are eleven all told, but really only eight do very much hunting. These eight are all scarred with the wounds they have received this very week in battling with the cougars and lynxes, and they are always threatening to fight one another; but they are as affectionate toward men (and especially toward me, as I pet them) as our own home dogs.

At this moment a large hound and a small half-bred bull-dog, both of which were quite badly wounded this morning by a cougar, are shoving their noses into my lap to be petted, and humming defiance to one another. They are on excellent terms with the ranch cat and kittens. The three chief fighting dogs, which do not follow the trail, are the most affectionate of all, and, moreover they climb trees!

Yesterday we got a big lynx in the top of a pinon tree—a low, spreading kind of pine—about thirty feet tall. Turk, the bloodhound followed him up and after much sprawling actually got to the very top, within a couple of feet of him. Then, when the lynx was shot out of the tree, Turk, after a short scramble, took a header down through the branches, landing with a bounce on his back. Tony, one of the half-breed bull-dogs, takes such headers on an average at least once for every animal we put up a tree. We have nice little horses which climb the most extraordinary places you can imagine. Get Mother to show you some of Gustave Dore's trees; the trees on these mountains look just like them.

The APBT in Literature

Several writers chronicled the versatile APBT. Ernest Thomas Seton, well-known nature writer, captures the clown inside the APBT in his short story, "The Making of Silly Billy," in which a boisterous and playful puppy on a remote mountain ranch sheds his puppyhood and his comedic qualities when he has to help the ranch owner battle a stock-killing bear. The young dog, when called upon to do so, shows his innate gameness and courage and

comes to the aid of the ranch hound pack in the process.

Jack London, in *White Fang*, amply illustrated what can happen to a dog (or a wolf-dog) when it confronts a pit bull in battle. Though White Fang, in London's fictional account, had battled dozens of other dogs (and wolves), his last adversary soundly defeated him. Only the intercession of the man who would come to own the wolf-dog saved White Fang from death from a hard-gripping pit veteran.

Mascots

Many colleges like the University of Georgia adopted the Bulldog as their mascot and intercollegiate identity. The squat and pushed-faced Bulldog of English fame may be the logo for these schools today, but it was the APBT, the "fighting bulldog," that the schools wanted to emulate in fighting prowess and grit. And the U.S. Marine Corps has adopted the ABPT as its official mascot.

The Quest for the Best

The pit dog breeders were a competitive lot and obtaining the best fighting dog, or the best sire or dam of winning dogs became not just a goal, but an absolute obsession. Old breed books cite famous breeders and the families of pit dogs they had developed. Famous dogs, usually multiple fight winners, were in great demand as stud dogs, with the owners of likely females coming from hundreds of miles to breed to the top studs.

Bitches that had won several fights were highly sought after as brood matrons to mate to great males in hopes of producing an even greater pit dog in their off-spring. Some farmers who were skilled pit dog breeders found the greatest crops they produced were the pups they sold to aspiring dog fighters or hopeful dog breeders.

Famous kennels sprang up in the South, the Midwest, the Northeast, and on the West Coast. French-named breeders from Louisiana found kindred spirits in Irish New Englanders, Scandinavian North Dakotans, Texas cowboys, Pittsburgh steelworkers, and Detroit auto builders. That kindred spirit was the American Pit Bull Terrier. The emerging APBT became emblematic of the American melting pot. Admirers of these dogs might have little else in common beyond a love and passion for their pit fighting bulldogs.

The American pit dog began to take on a different look from the British dogs of the Staffordshire Bull Terrier mold. American dogs were usually somewhat taller. The essence of the pit dog was not, however, in his outward appearance. Many fighting traits might be sought after in a planned mating of two great dogs, but above all other attributes was the oft-misunderstood element of "gameness." Gameness became and remains the credo of many APBT breeders today.

Gameness

Gameness is not a dog's courage, fighting ability, or even endurance. Gameness is the never quit, fight-to-the-death personality of what are called "game-bred" pit bulls. Game dogs were not necessarily the best fighters, but they were the dogs with the most fight in them. Gameness made a 30-pound (14 kg) pit bull able to take on much larger adversaries, especially in other breeds, and ultimately triumph. Other kinds of canines might be slashing and damaging fighters for short spans of time. Other breeds might possess great size and strength and be absolutely devastating against non-pit dogs. One rancher-owner of Irish Wolfhounds told how a young male dog of that breed, standing 37 inches (94 cm) at the shoulder, was attacked by several feral dogs and left most of his attackers dead or dying. But fighting skill alone does not a pit dog make.

Breeding the Best to the Best

Holding to their view that the APBT is the "original bulldog," pit dog men bought the best of the best British lines. They bought the small, inbred, red, red-nosed Irish dog; the larger Blue Pauls (or Polls) of Scotland, and representatives of the Staffordshire Bull type before they were molded in an exhibition direction. Taking this broad spectrum of imported bloodlines, but holding to the vision that they were deal-ing with the original bulldog, APBT breeders applied the rapidly growing skills of dog breeding.

They followed the generally accepted practice of breeding the best to the best, with the pit serving as the ultimate testing ground that proved just which dog was best. No sentimentality or color prefer-ences were applicable; the best dog was the only dog left stand-ing. The only attributes admired, and sought in breeding stock, were those attributes that contributed to pit success. Winners and their near kin were inbred, linebred, and out-crossed on other winners, but pit ability was the overriding obsession that kept this interest alive.

Using only a rudimentary knowl-edge of genetics, legendary breed-ers laid a foundation of a single purpose—gameness in the dog pit. While the APBT might be an excellent pet and companion, an able stock dog, or a great help for game hunters, these roles were always secondary to the rigid requirements of the pit. Using this single measuring stick, the pit dog breeders maximized these abilities. They built them into every success-ful pit dog and then they bred only the most suc-cessful pit dogs. The hon-ing and polishing of the American Pit Bull Terrier went on for generation after generation.

"Made in America"

The United States has always been a nation of improvers. The Thoroughbred horse may have originated in England, but horseracing and racehorses reached new heights in America. As Britain went in another direction with the rootstock of the APBT, Americans bred this same rootstock to its ultimate genetic conclusion. The ancestors of today's Staffordshire Bull Terrier are also the ancestors of the APBT, but the squatty Staffordshire Bull Terrier show dog of the modern show ring has only vague similarity to the APBT. Even a casual observer can easily see that they are different breeds. The Staffordshire Bull Terrier is an English creation; the APBT developed on this side of the Atlantic.

Dog breeders did not sculpt the APBT with particular visual ideals in mind, as had been the case with James Hinks' Bull Terrier, which also originated in England. Hinks endeavored to produce a beautiful, athletic dog with a unique appearance using the ancestors of the Staffordshire Bull Terrier, the Dalmatian, and probably the Spanish Pointer.

He clearly succeeded in creating a show dog with great beauty and uniformity. His breed was enormously popular in England, but it was not simply a pit dog in a tuxedo.

The APBT started from some of the same origins: the pit dogs of the British Isles. Breeding took an opposite turn in the United States. The appearance of the pit dogs here was of no great import. In the words of an Irish immigrant who brought his pit dogs with him, "The best color for a fighting dog is winning." While many APBTs looked different from one another externally, most possessed the same internal fire. Even

when pit fighting was more or less an underground activity, dogs of this breed were, to varying degrees, still considered game-bred.

The intense pressure that dog breeding can exert has negatively impacted some breeds. The once useful and beautiful Irish Setter has seen his beauty maximized while his usefulness has been minimized. The Collie, in a quest for show beauty, lost much of his original shepherding prowess to the not-as-beautiful Border Collie. The American Cocker Spaniel once comprised 25 percent of the dogs in America. Cocker breeders now recognize that this great popularity did the breed much more harm than good.

The APBT was an American variation on a British theme. For many decades, the goals of all pit dog people were the same. The breed was given one primary task, a task it performed better than any other breed that has ever existed. Americans took great pride in bringing this breed to its ultimate refinement.

The Ultimate Canine Fighting Machine

The APBT, as a breed, is the best fighting dog in the world. Though some individual dogs of similar breeds have bested individual pit bulls on rare occasions, there is no breed that can even hope to compete with the APBT in the fighting pit. The stubby Staffordshire, the elegant Bull Terrier, the Japanese Akita, and the Chinese Shar-pei can't do it. Even the massive Tosa Inu can't do it. All of these breeds, and others, have been matched against the APBT and have most often been beaten.

Over the centuries, since humans have matched dogs against one another, the APBT and its ancestors were bred for this task. They excelled in fighting. They liked fighting. Fighting was the reason for their existence. Dogs of other breeds can be trained to fight other dogs. The APBT doesn't have to be trained.

A pit dog can be conditioned into shape for fighting. Some trainers believe they can enhance the way a dog fights with certain exercises and gimmicks, but only in minor ways. Pit dogs fight because it is part of what they are.

Fighting for a pit dog is not the same as fighting for a Malamute, a German Shepherd Dog, a Rottweiler, or a Doberman. Most other breeds bristle and put on aggressive displays. If the potential opponent submits to this show of force, a fight can usually be avoided. Pit dogs don't spend much time on displays; they simply walk up, fight until the opponent is incapacitated or dead, and move on. Fighting is not a ritual or even a defense mechanism for pit dogs. Fighting for such dogs is a way of life.

Other breeds may be terrible to behold when they are fighting. Their owners may tout their canine's "killer instincts." Some extol their dogs' fighting styles. Perhaps these owners are correct about the dominance of their non-pit dogs over other *similar* dogs. Other breeds simply cannot stand close fighting scrutiny when paired with an APBT. Other breeds have heritages that have been structured for some other work: herding, guarding, hunting, and so on. The work of the pit dog is to fight! Centuries of breeding for gameness, high pain tolerance, powerful jaws, and a muscular physique, combine with a single-minded focus to make the APBT the ultimate fighting breed.

Chapter Four

Dogfighting and Dogfighters

Why Even Discuss Dogfighting?

Dogfighting to most Americans is a terrible thing. To most of our society, dogfighting is more repugnant than many crimes against human beings. Dogfighting seems to be a throwback to a more barbaric time when life was cheap, especially animal life. Dogfighting is a crime in most of the civilized world. Why then, even in a book on the American Pit Bull Terrier, would a discussion of dogfighting be appropriate? The answer is incredibly simple: Unless you understand dogfighting—whatever your opinions about dogfighting may be—you cannot truly understand the breed that was bred to excel at it.

So much invective has been spewed about this breed and its heritage that reality for many has been lost in a flood of acrimony. Including a chapter on this activity and the people who engaged—and, unfortunately, still engage—in it with APBTs is the only way to give readers a chance to separate truth from fiction for themselves. By knowing the truth,

perhaps we can effectively extricate a grossly misunderstood and vilified dog breed from the activity that created that breed.

Author's Note: This chapter is not a treatise on why dogfighting is a good thing. I am trying to write a book that will provide you with a fair and unbiased view of the APBT. Bred for the pit, the APBT cannot be assessed as a breed without an understanding of that same pit. Much of the stigma heaped on the APBT comes from widely disseminated misinformation about just how pit dogs and dog pits functioned. Dog fighting is illegal. I believe in obeying the law. The right APBT in the right hands is an excellent animal companion. Whether you want to believe this or not, *the dog pit that shaped the pit bull also imbued the dog with some of its best qualities*. It is appropriate to be against organized pit dogfighting, but I don't believe it is appropriate to castigate an entire breed in so doing.

The accent in this chapter will be on understanding this truth about dogfighting in order to give a more accurate view of the conditions under which the APBT developed.

The Ultimate Selection Process

Most animal breeding activities have clear and ever-present goals that serve as a template or guide for breeders. Thoroughbred horseracing resulted in a breed of spirited horses with speed and endurance. Heavy armor worn by medieval knights

required a different kind of horse, a large and heavy animal without the thoroughbred's speed. Though both were horses that carried riders on their backs, the goals were different and the horses developed differently.

In dogs, selection for traits has resulted in an estimated 600 different breeds throughout the world. Experts now generally agree that all dogs sprang from essentially the same genetic source, the wolf. Given that wolves in different environments may have minor differences in their appearance cannot account for the great diversity in the dogs of today. Humans, through selective breeding, have been able to mold the canine into an amazing group of quite different-looking animals that are all still dogs. Two factors are always at work in the breeding of animals: selection for certain factors, and culling or disposing of those individuals that don't have those required factors.

Earlier chapters on the heritage and history of the APBT have shown the early factors that went into the selection processes that created the mastiffs, the bulldogs, the terriers, the bull-and-terrier breeds, and ultimately the APBT. Much of this history and heritage has involved animal fighting and the "blood sports." The element of danger to dogs that were set on much larger animals and then set on other dogs created one of the selection factors.

Other selection factors gradually surfaced and took precedence over previous requirements. The large mastiff breeds that fought in wars against men and then in the arena against every kind of wild animal gave way to the smaller bulldogs that participated in the bullbaiting contests. When bullbaiting was no longer a feasible recreation, smaller and faster bulldog and bull-and-terrier types were matched against one another. These matches became more and more intense. This intensity found its way into breeding the dogs that became the APBT.

Selection

Selection for the pit fighting dogs was always quite focused. The process left off such niceties as color, hair length, exaggerated appearance, or abnormal size. The pit concerned selection only for gameness and fighting. Any attributes that did not directly and immediately contribute to success in the pit were sloughed off. Ultimately, the resulting pit dog was a medium-sized, athletic, shorthaired animal with great determination, a high pain threshold, and a no-quit attitude. The only cosmetic affectation was the cropping of a pit dog's ears for pit rather than appearance purposes. The pit bull was not the only fighting dog breed in the world, but it proved to be the absolute best.

Culling

The second part of the duality in animal breeding, the culling (or discarding) process took on a rigid and harsh tone. Quite simply, a dog

that did not survive in the pit obviously never made it to the breeding pen. This same axiom proved true in gamecocks and homing pigeons. Gamecocks that died early in the cockpit never had an opportunity to replicate their kind for the future of cockfighting, and homing pigeons that couldn't find their way home didn't have the chance to pass along this trait to their descendants. Rather than a simplistic statement, the alternative to success for the pit dog was death.

In other kinds of dogs, rejects might be foisted off on the unknowing next buyer, they might be sold as pets, or they might be given away. Often, poor-quality dogs in almost every breed did get an opportunity to breed and they reproduced poorer-quality dogs in a cycle that nearly destroyed a number of once great breeds. Historically, this did not happen with pit dogs. If the dog pit didn't finish the poor-quality dog, the pit dog breeder usually did. In either case, the potential for this dog to spread his poor quality ended with the death of this dog.

As harsh as the pit's culling may have been, it was sure and it was certain. Viewed from the perspective of the quest of a specific dog-breeding goal, it was also profoundly successful. Poor-quality dogs were immediately eliminated from consideration as future breeding stock. Many fights between equally matched canine battlers did not result in the death of either dog when both animals proved their gameness and worth as possible progenitors of pit dogs. Stopping a fight often salvaged worthy losers. The win and prize purse went to the winning dog's owner; respect and a reputation for gameness went to both dogs.

Fight-winning males and females (or their close kin) formed the nucleus of the breeding stock to produce the next generation of dogs that would ultimately become known as APBTs. The gameness that made these dogs able to endure hours of pain in a pit often showed itself in some of the progeny of the successive generations. While some poorer-quality pit dogs may have been allowed to breed, the important stud dogs and brood bitches of the breed were generally pit-tested veterans. Sometimes an injury or some other minor problem would keep a dog out of the pit. Such a dog would be proved as a quality breeder by the prowess of sons and daughters in pit fights.

Human sensibilities notwithstanding, the dog pits did their work, and did it clearly. When dogs are bred

for battle, the only way that they can be truly tested is in battle. Abhorrent as they may have been, the pits made a definite contribution to the quality of the dogs that fought in them. The pits were a tough test that only the best fighting dogs could overcome.

A Sometimes Illegal Activity

Even in the early days of bull-baiting and dogfighting, most of the population was not in attendance. In England, and later in the United States, most of the population was either oblivious to dogfighting or turned a blind eye to its existence. Dogfighters, pit dog breeders, gamblers, and the retinue of hangers-on who preyed on the gamblers—prostitutes, sycophants, muggers, and creditors—made up much of the audience at dogfights. There were also the morbidly curious, the thrill-seekers, and the sadistic elements of the community. There were the businesspeople who owned the pits or openly or secretly owned one (or both) of the contestants. There were also people who greatly loved seeing the APBT doing what it was bred to do.

Dogfighting was a misdemeanor in many places in the U.S. over the years but did not become a felony until 1976, when it was outlawed by federal law. Dogfighting did not cease to exist with criminalization, but it did become harder to openly conduct and follow. There were still magazines that published fight results, but never the exact locations of where the fights took place. Advertisers continued to support these magazines, and in the time between the imposing of misdemeanor status in many areas and federal felony status, dogfighting continued to flourish.

Gone were the days when fights were advertised in daily newspapers and with handbills and posters plastered on every wall, pole, and tree. The fighters became highly selective in their acquaintances and in those allowed to attend matches.

Already made up of a rather tight circle of people, dogfighting became even more clannish and exclusive. Even though some law enforcement officials were paid to look the other way, as penalties grew for dogfighting, so did the possibility of long jail sentences impact on many fighters. Breeders and admirers of the APBT did not become paranoid until felony status was accorded dogfighting. The possibility of some serious jail time and a growing humane movement drove thousands from any active participation in pit dogs or dog pits.

Some Myths About Why Dogs Fight

The public outcry over "those terrible pit bulls" and over dogfighting that has come to the fore in the past several decades has brought countless "dog experts" to the surface. Some of these experts are well intentioned but ignorant about APBTs, in particular; others are only seeking a forum for their views and for notoriety. Still others have a stack of agendas, which may or may not have much to do with the APBT. Some supposed authorities look like fighting dogs themselves battling for the spotlight, the camera, and the attention of the media. Some of these people are politically motivated; some seem to be seeking a cause to espouse. Others have what they feel is an open-and-shut issue that may produce public exposure and photo ops.

Because most of this group knows nothing about the special circumstances surrounding APBTs, a number of myths have sprung up around the APBT, and a gullible or negligent media often picks up and spreads wrong information garnered from these various self-styled "accurate sources."

Even today, when the street pit dogfighters clearly have no interest in their dogs or in public safety, they don't suffer much for their felony crimes. Plea bargaining, political influence, and turning state's evidence can allow a flagrant violator back on the street, or even back in the pit, in a few days, weeks, or months. Conversely, most of the dogs confiscated at a fight, or at an alleged fighter's home, are seen as "enemies of the state" and as liabilities to the community at large, and are ultimately euthanized. The pit dogs, unlike most APBTs that are rescued by organizations, aren't usually easy to put up for adoption, so often they too are euthanized.

The "dreaded pit bulls" are killed, but only after their pictures—usually in the most biased poses—are slathered across the front pages of newspapers and on TV screens. The general public is thus given another false view of APBTs. Reporters write what they believe is the case: that the public is better off with these dogs dead and forgotten.

Are APBTs Trained to Fight?

One myth about APBTs is that they have to be trained to fight. Laws have even been written with this training nonsense prominently threaded through them. APBTs can be conditioned physically, just as sled dogs, Greyhounds, and even police dogs for the rigors of the pit. Most people who are really familiar with the breed believe that you can no more train such dogs to fight than you can train a cat to catch mice.

Generation after generation of intense breeding of dogs bred specifically to fight need little or no enhancement. While many APBTs are not inordinately aggressive toward other dogs, even toward other APBTs, a safe bet is to believe that a high percentage will be. Some of these can be effectively socialized or trained or controlled so that they never become a problem. I have been in the presence of three female canines that were visiting in a pet store: an APBT, an Ameri-

can Bulldog, and a wolf-dog hybrid. All three were well mannered and soon stretched out side by side for a communal snooze, to the gasps of passersby. All three had been carefully socialized, were well trained, and under the watchful (and controlling) eyes of their three owners.

Are APBTs Normally Human-Aggressive?

Animal-aggressive behavior is present in many dogs of every size and sort. Jack Russell Terriers, for example, and other terriers have this attribute in great amounts, perhaps even more than many modern APBTs. The strength and power of the APBT heightens the need for owner awareness and care regarding any aggressive behavior. When properly socialized as a very young puppy, an APBT can grow to be a quite peaceable pet. Alert owners can keep such a dog under appropriate control and protect it from any involvement that could lead to a fight.

Animal aggression does not equate with human aggression. Dogs most certainly can be trained to be aggressive toward humans; the traditional pit dog was not. APBTs in the hands of sane, reasonable, and caring owners will not usually be human-aggressive. The breed is not naturally aggressive toward people and therefore is not naturally a very effective guard dog against human intruders. This statement may fly in the face of conventional wisdom, but understanding how traditional dog-

fights were conducted gives a clear explanation of why this is so.

The unknowing have always accepted the idea that pit dogs are mean and vicious killers. Viciousness is often mentioned along with aggressive behavior in news stories about pit dogs. What is not written and not said is that the pit dogs, in organized fights conducted under established rules, were dog-aggressive, not vicious. The fact that these same APBTs were the sires and dams of the next generation and that this happened over many generations assured that the breed itself would not be human-aggressive. So much for the American Pit Bull Terrier being an automatic danger to human beings.

Dogfighting was and still is a very rugged and dangerous activity for the dogs. Some dogs were horribly scarred and maimed. Other dogs were killed in the pit or died from their injuries. That much is true. It is also true that many dogfights did not end in the death of either dog. In some early books and magazines on the "pit bull" or on the APBT, some pit dogs' win and lost records are given. It is not uncommon to see a dog with several wins and several losses retired to become a stud dog or a brood bitch.

Game pit fighting dogs were a valuable commodity. If a losing dog had demonstrated that it was brave and that it was willing to keep fighting though outmatched on a particular occasion, most owners would be understandably reluctant to lose such a dog in a prolonged fight after the outcome was obvious. A game loser was cheered and revered almost as much as a fight winner. Cowardly, clumsy, and inept fighters probably would not have been spared.

Rules and Regulations

For many years, pit fights were conducted under a rigid set of regulations. Two dogs were matched (paired up to size, age, and experience) and their owners brought their dogs to the actual pit area. Under the watchful eyes of the referee and spectators, the owners exchanged dogs. Each owner (or his second) then washed the other owner's dog to be certain that nothing had been applied to either dog's coat to discourage biting and mouthing from its pit opponent. This practice, a part of pit regimen for over 100 years, impacted on the pit dog's lack of aggressiveness toward human beings. A dog that, because of aggressiveness toward humans, couldn't be handled or washed by its opponent's owner couldn't be fought under pit rules. A vicious man-hater could not be trusted, would not be fought, and would never become the ancestor of other dogs that might share the same problem disposition.

In a fight, the dogs were brought to a scratch line across the pit from one another. Each would be released and would fight until one dog "turned" or avoided contact. At a turn, a break would be called and each owner would pick up his dog and treat the dog much the way cornermen handle human boxers between rounds in a boxing match.

Imagine, for a moment that you are the owner of one of the dogs. He has been fighting for his life and is probably injured by this time and you have to pick up the injured dog and give him some brief care. If you have ever picked up an injured dog of any breed, the potential for being bitten is greater at this time than at any other time in a dog's life. That is true for most dogs, but it simply did not happen often in dog pits. A dog that could not be handled by its owner, even though badly hurt, would never be allowed to reproduce and probably wouldn't make it home from the fight alive in any case.

To more fully understand the APBT, it is important to recognize that the traditional dog fights that took place in Ireland, England, and the United States weren't casual affairs. These fights were not simply the random tossing of two dogs into a ring and allowing them to kill each other. The rules were clearly delineated and rule breakers were punished and eventually ostracized. Sometimes huge sums of money were wagered on the outcomes of these fights. Each side insisted on rules that kept the fight as honest as possible.

Think what you will about pit dog fighting, but realize that some aspects of the pit experience that branded the APBT were positive. No other breed has had to be held to such an exacting standard. Not only did the APBT have to be game unto

death, he had to be safe for humans to be around under the lights and arenalike atmosphere of the dog pit. When someone loudly asserts that the American Pit Bull Terrier, because of his pit heritage, is a canine menace to the community at large, the truth simply doesn't support this view.

The Dogfighters

Just as it is not accurate to lump every APBT into one group, so it is not accurate to put all dogfighters into one category. Dogfighting, in one form or another, has been going on for centuries. There seem to be two primary types of dogfighters. These two types, regardless of how one feels about dogfighting, are poles apart. One type could be called the traditionalists; the other could accurately be described as thugs. One group, as repugnant as we may find their activities, was concerned about the dogs and fought according to rigid rules. To the other groups, the welfare of the dogs meant nothing and rules were nonexistent.

Traditional Dogfighters

Traditional dogfighters were usually dog breeders as well as pit dog owners. These individuals were skilled in choosing the right APBTs to mate to produce a line or family of game fighting dogs. They were also skilled in developing "keeps" or exercise and nutritional regimens to condition their fighters. Many traditional fighters became known for their own lines of APBTs. Because of the success of their dogs in the pit, these owner-breeder-fighters were sought after for their extra puppies or the occasional breeding or fighting adult.

APBTs were often identified by their owner's name, such as "Smith's Red Flash" or "Brown's Jug." Traditional APBT people were usually quite protective of their reputations and acted accordingly in their dealings involving their dogs. From the early days up to today, the name of a respected breeder adds value to a dog. In turn, a good dog bearing a breeder's name enhances that individual as well.

It was the dog-breeding skill of these traditionalists and the carefully (and often secretly) maintained pedigrees that created the American Pit Bull Terrier as a breed. The traditionalists' holding to strict breeding and fighting rules made the APBT strong and healthy when other purebred dogs suffered from an overdependence on inbreeding. Other breeds won public attention, became fads, peaked, and went out of favor. The APBT, especially in the tight circle of true fans, remains much the same as it did 100 years ago.

Though the traditional fighters contested their dogs in dog pits, they seemed to truly care about their dogs. They gave them good care, good food, and good housing. To do otherwise for a pit dog was to decrease his chances to be a winner in the pit. Many traditional breeders kept retired fighters that were past breeding age and treated them as beloved house pets. They provided veterinary care, and many former pit dogs lived out their lives with the very persons who had risked these same lives in numerous pit appearances.

Though carefully hidden from public view, some traditionalists still take their APBTs to pits and fight them today. It is safe to say that none of the higher-echelon individuals engaged in this activity is likely to be incarcerated or charged for it. Newcomers, the not very bright, the careless, the lazy, the trusting, and the unlucky are most likely to suffer a felony conviction for dogfighting. Much like the pit dogs themselves, today's traditional dogfighter seems to want to show gameness in the face of increasing public sentiment, felony crime status, and vastly improved law enforcement. At a time when traditional dogfighting should be the stuff of history books, it appears that traditional dogfighting is flying in the face of the prevailing trends against it.

The Other Dogfighters

The other group of dogfighters are irresponsible individuals who care nothing for the breed or for the individual dogs; they are more prevalent today. They are generally career criminal types who see dogfighting as a sort of canine crap game. They follow no rules and will impulsively fight their dogs at any time. One street punk admitted that he fought his brood bitch against another pit, even though his dog was nursing a litter of seven-week-old puppies!

Many of these irresponsible individuals own pit-type dogs only so that they can walk around with a tough-looking canine and appear more menacing themselves. Most of the dogs that these quasi-tough guys own are poorly bred, bad specimens with uncertain heritages and really can't be considered APBTs at all. They are human-aggressive street dogs and have been trained for viciousness by their vicious owners. Most of the attacks on children and other humans that can be legitimately attributed to "pit bulls" are from this kind of misbegotten dog. Not only are these animals dangerous, but their owners are often dangerous as well.

In an interview, a breeder of APBTs regularly acknowledged that his dogs were indeed animal-aggressive and couldn't be trusted around other dogs. He also stated that any stranger who wanted to come into his kennel area would be perfectly safe and he recently has had two APBTs stolen from his backyard to validate this statement.

APBTs, or any other dogs, don't belong in the hands of the ignorant, stupid, irresponsible, or malicious, but it is just this group that seems to own an inordinately large number of what could be called "pit bulls." The fear and loathing that has been heaped on the true APBT rightfully belongs to this group. Thugs and punks have been allowed to change the basic focus of public understanding of an exceptional breed, the American Pit Bull Terrier.

The modern traditional fighters have nothing to do with the street pit punks; they won't sell them dogs and they won't give them any help. True traditionalists won't breed their stud dog to a street pit bitch. If a street punk casually assumes that because he and the traditional dogfighter both have dogs, and that makes them friends, nothing could be further from the truth. In the words of one friend of the APBT, "Equating the gangs and thugs that fight dogs in alleys and vacant buildings with the true Pit Bull Terrier enthusiasts is like making some connection between a baseball player who earns his living swinging a bat and a mugger who makes his living also swinging a bat."

Chapter Five

The APBT and the Dog Registries

Registries, usually in the form of kennel clubs, brought standardization to the world of purebred dog breeding. Kennel clubs are composed of delegates from a number of breed clubs and similar organizations. They are never static. They have new members coming in and old members going out every year. Kennel clubs take some heat for their actions, but as these actions relate to the various breeds, kennel clubs must take their lead from the actions and desires of the separate breed clubs that oversee their respective breeds.

It is easy to castigate the American Kennel Club, for example, for failing to accept the APBT and opting instead for the oddly named (considering historical reality) Staffordshire Terrier. Though I have pointed at the AKC on more than one occasion, the American Kennel Club did not treat the APBT unfairly. The breeders who accepted the Staffordshire appellation did not treat the APBT unfairly. In the cold light of fact, most breeders of the APBT in the mid-1930s

never wanted to be connected with the American Kennel Club. Nobody actually mistreated anybody!

The minority of breeders who, some 60-odd years ago, wanted to be involved with conformation dog shows with their APBTs were able to do just that. They developed a breed club and accepted the AKC sentiment that the word "pit" should be taken out of the breed's name. The Bull Terrier (the long-faced white and colored "Spuds McKenzie" dogs) protested that the name "American Bull Terrier" was too near their own. Grasping at the only halfway reasonable name, the APBT, for AKC purposes, became the Staffordshire Terrier and later became the American Staffordshire Terrier.

Without kennel clubs and breed registries, the dog-buying public would be even more at the mercies of puppy-mill charlatans and the "breed-for-greed" crowd. Cumbersome, they sometimes are. Bureaucratic, they often are. Necessary, they *always* are.

Dog Registries Affecting the APBT

Dog registries add legitimacy to dog-breeding efforts. Before there were organized dog-registering organizations, there was always a cloud over the pedigree offered as evidence of a particular dog's heritage from one dog owner to another. The Kennel Club in England, the American Kennel Club, the United Kennel Club, and the American Dog Breeders Association all gave a stamp of approval to purebred dogs. Registries help assure that a particular dog is really what he appears to be, both in reality and on paper.

The APBT in England

The registration path followed by the pit dog in England—the Staffordshire Bull Terrier—and the pit dog in the United States—the APBT—is remarkably similar. In Britain, game-bred dogs had been a part of the

canine landscape for 500 years. These dogs were carefully bred to a strict code of requirements, but this code was usually unwritten and kept only in the minds of dogfighters. Though clearly a specific breed type, the dogs that today are England's most popular terriers, the Staffordshire Bull Terriers, were viewed, by some, as a ragtag collection of mongrels. In 1935 a breed club was formed for "The Original Staffordshire Bull Terrier." This name was viewed unfavorably by the Bull Terrier breeders. The Bull Terrier was a much more popular breed at the time, and yet a much younger breed. The English Kennel Club did not approve this name until the word "Original" was dropped from their name.

Breeders of the Bull Terrier certainly protested the name of this "new" terrier. This is ironic because the pit dogs of Staffordshire made up the major part of the ancestry of the Bull Terrier. Gradually England's pit terrier—the Staffordshire Bull Terrier, the ancestor of America's pit terrier, the APBT, gained acceptance, and in 1948 began to grow in registry numbers.

The APBT in the United States

In the United States, the American Kennel Club accepted the APBT into its organization in 1936, but not under that name. Because of the pit connotation, the AKC accepted the name "Staffordshire Terrier" for the APBT. The shakiness of the logic in choosing this name came to the

surface in 1972 when the Staffordshire Bull Terrier from the English KC sought admission into the AKC. It would have been cumbersome and confusing to have the "Staffordshire Terrier" and the "Staffordshire Bull Terrier" in the same organization. The breeders chose "American Staffordshire Terrier" to further differentiate one breed from the other. The AKC registered the Amstaff in 1936 and the Staffy Bull has been registered since 1972. Two other registries—the United Kennel Club (1898) and the American Dog Breeders Association (1909)—had already recognized the APBT for decades.

C. Z. Bennett and the United Kennel Club

The nineteenth century saw dogfighting become a popular pasttime first in urban centers and then in other locales in the still-growing United States. By the 1850s dogfighters were well ensconced in America. Cargo ships plying the Atlantic were regularly bringing pit dogs from both England and Ireland, and American dog breeders began to see the potential in these fighting dogs.

Bulldogs and bull-and-terrier dogs were becoming popular in the United States. At the same time that the progenitors of the APBT were arriving, the ancestors of the Boston Terrier also made the scene. In the remaining years of the century, through the Civil War, Reconstruction, and all the other events that contributed to the growth of the country, dog breeders were developing the APBT. While breeders kept careful records and pedigrees, these were usually kept secret. Gameness and other pit attributes were the breeding goals. Some dogs were large, some were small, some were solid-colored, some were spotted. Some dogs were thickly muscled and broad chested; others were slimmer and rangier.

Into this welter of nondescript pit dogs came a man of far-reaching vision, Chauncy Z. Bennett. In 1898, seeing the need for an organization for his favorite breed, Bennett founded the United Kennel Club. The older American Kennel Club at that time wanted nothing to do with what one early AKC official referred to as "pit fighting mongrels." Bennett sorted through all the names for the pit terriers: Half-and-Half, American Bullterrier, Yankee Terrier, and so forth. He settled on the name American (Pit) Bull Terrier, though later the parentheses were removed.

The United Kennel Club, which is today the country's second largest dog registry with over 200 breeds recognized, was the first organization to grant recognition to the pit dogs that became the APBT. C. Z. Bennett wrote the first standard, which is a written description of what the ideal dog should look like, of the breed. He also drew up rules and regulations about dogfighting and the dog pits. He brought organization to this activity and a semblance of respectability for the breed, if not for the fighting. If he did not actually create the APBT in flesh and bone, Bennett did give them acceptance and transformed a group of sometimes quite dissimilar dogs into what would become one of the best-known dog breeds in the history of the world.

The United Kennel Club of today has absolutely no connection with any dogfighting activities or any other illegal or inhumane activities. Building on their early success with the APBT, the UKC became the registry for most of the Coonhound breeds in the United States and other American breeds that were disavowed by, ignored by, or unknown to the AKC. Today's United Kennel Club still maintains its ties with the APBT and also recognizes the AKC's version of the APBT, the American Staffordshire Terrier. UKC conformation shows and other events are held throughout the United States every week of the year.

Others have extended the official olive branch of sanctioning and recognition to the APBT in the years since 1898, but C. Z. Bennett and the United Kennel Club did it first. By providing a framework for standardization for the APBT, Bennett brought the benefits of name recognition. Dogfighters and fans of the pit dogs had traditionally just called them "bulldogs," and many of them still do today, which led to confusion for the general public.

The United Kennel Club Standard for the APBT

Head: The head should be medium length and bricklike in shape. The skill is flat and widest at the ears, with prominent cheeks free from wrinkles.

Muzzle: The muzzle is square, wide and deep. Well-pronounced jaws should display strength. The upper teeth should meet tightly over the lower teeth, outside on front.

Ears: The ears are cropped or uncropped (not important) and should be set high on the head, free from wrinkles.

Eyes: The round eyes should be set far apart, low down on the skull. Any color is acceptable.

Nose: The nose should have wide open nostrils. Any color is acceptable.

Neck: Muscular and slightly arched, the neck should taper from shoulder to head, free from looseness of skin.

Shoulders: The shoulders should be strong and muscular, with wide sloping shoulder blades.

Back: Short and strong, the back should slightly slope from the withers to the rump. It should be slightly arched at the loins which should be slightly tucked.

Chest: The chest should be deep, but not too broad, with wide sprung ribs.

Ribs: Close. Well sprung, with deep back ribs.

Tail: Short in comparison to size, the tail should be set low and tapering to a fine point. It should not be carried over the back. A bobbed tail is not acceptable.

Legs: The legs should be large and round boned, with straight, upright pasterns, reasonably strong. The feet should be of medium size. The gait should be light and springy, with no rolling or pacing.

Thigh: The thigh should be long with muscles developed and hocks down straight.

Coat: The coat should be glossy, and short and stiff to the touch.

Color: Any color or markings are permissible.

Weight: The weight is not important. The preferred weight for females is from 30 to 50 pounds (13.6–22.7 kg), for males from 35 to 60 pounds (15.9–27.2 kg).

The American Dog Breeders Association

In 1909, eleven years after C. Z. Bennett founded the United Kennel Club, Guy McCord began the American Dog Breeders Association, Inc. (ADBA) as an exclusive association for APBT breeders. McCord was a close friend of one of the legends in pit dog fame, John P. Colby, and a staunch supporter of the breed. Early documents give the precise goals of the organization and a realistic view of conditions for the APBT at the turn of the century. This material is printed by permission of the ADBA.

The APBT is now recognized as a standard breed, where a few years ago, it was unrecognized as a breed. The majority of the American public carried the impression that the APBT was synonymous with dogs used for fighting purposes only. This idea has been dispelled by persistent efforts of the breeders who compose this association. Presently, classes for APBTs can be found at almost every local dog show being held. With concerted effort, our faithful friend will in time be classed as the leading American dog, who will give his life if necessary in defense of his master/mistress. We trust that you will unite with us in our efforts to bring this dog to the destiny he deserves.

While things didn't exactly work out just in that manner, the ADBA brought another view to the sponsorship of the APBT. Today, the ADBA continues to be the lead registration for the APBT. This organization, located in Salt Lake City, Utah, holds conformation dog shows and weight-pulling matches for the only breed it registers—the APBT.

In 1976 the ADBA wanted a standard for the APBT, but did not want just a restatement of the UKC standard for the APBT or the AKC standard for the American Staffordshire Terrier.

The Basis of Conformation for the APBT was the ADBA's carefully considered response to the standards developed by the AKC for the American Staffordshire Terrier and by the UKC for the APBT. This Basis of Conformation is too lengthy and detailed for inclusion here, but the author encourages anyone with a sincere interest in this breed to write to the ADBA (see Useful Addresses and Literature, page 170) or go to this organization's web site on the Internet. The American Dog Breeders are only concerned with the

APBT and are an excellent resource for anyone who wants to really understand this breed.

The American Staffordshire Terrier

Fearful of what primarily breeding just for conformation might do to their breed, most of the APBT breeders in 1935 did not want their dogs in the AKC. The United Kennel Club did not yet have conformation shows, as both they and the ADBA now do, and some APBT people wanted to be able to show their pets in AKC shows. Under the name of the Staffordshire Terrier, a group petitioned the AKC and was admitted in 1935. As has been mentioned, the name was changed to American Staffordshire Terrier in 1972 with the admission of the original pit dog of them all, the Staffordshire Bull Terrier.

Are APBTs and Amstaffs the Same Breed?

The AKC allowed APBTs to be registered as Amstaffs for a number of years until the studbook was closed. This meant that from the closing of the studbook on, the AKC would register only dogs whose parents were registered as American Staffordshire Terriers. Since that time, the Amstaff has gradually changed from what it had been as a renamed American Pit Bull Terrier. It is correct to state, in general terms, that the AKC Amstaff and the APBT of the UKC and ADBA is now not the same breed. They look quite similar, but there have been changes in the Amstaff after 65 years of breeding purely for conformation.

The differences between the Amstaff and the APBT would be even greater if there had not been dual registration. Some of the APBT breeders who opted for their dogs' inclusion in the American Kennel Club as Staffordshire Terriers and then as American Staffordshire Terriers, kept their dogs registered in the United Kennel Club as APBTs. There are still some dual-registered dogs today. Several years ago, the top APBT of the United Kennel Club was also the top American Staffordshire Terrier of the American Kennel Club! All claims and dramatic protestations to the contrary, in some cases, the Amstaff and the APBT are the same breed.

The Staffordshire Bull Terrier

The Staffordshire Bull Terrier—nicknamed "Stafford" or "Staffy Bull"—is currently the most popular terrier breed in England. The breed claims to be and probably is the lineal descendant of the original fighting terriers of England. Unfortunately, the Bulldog (called English Bulldog by some) claims to be the original lineal

descendant of the old bulldogs of England's bearbaiting and bullbaiting days. How different must the modern Bulldog look from its ancestors? How different must the modern Staffy Bull look from its ancestors? Though the Staffy Bull is a vigorous little terrier with loads of charm, the first word that often comes to mind about this breed is "cute." Somehow, the mental image of the fighting pit bull terrier being described as cute is bothersome. Somewhere in the years since pit dogfighting was banned in Britain, something happened to the Staffy Bull—not necessarily something bad, but certainly something! The "cute" Staffy Bull has been banned in dozens of places, probably solely because of the words "Staffordshire" and "Bull" in its name. If you have ever seen a Staffy Bull, banning Bambi seems more credulous!

The Bull Terrier (AKC)

Throughout this narrative, much has been made about what the Bull Terrier was or is *not.* It has been stated that the Bull Terrier is not the same as the "pit bull," the APBT, the American Staffordshire Terrier, or the Staffordshire Bull Terrier. So much for what the Bull Terrier *isn't.* The breed *is* a great many very positive things.

Forget about any comparisons as a fighting dog—either to the old-time Stafford or to the APBT—the Bull Terrier simply couldn't compete

in the pit. Where the Bull Terrier did compete, in the show ring, it did marvelously well. Though there have been many allusions to a fighting background, the Bull Terrier may be rough-and-tumble in a college touch football sort of way. The BT couldn't do what the pit-bred dogs do, because it was never a pit-bred dog. This is an excellent breed, with many of the qualities of the APBT, the Staffy Bull, and the Amstaff, but the Bull Terrier brings ample qualities all its own.

Chapter Six

Understanding the APBT

Gameness

In conversations with former dog-fighters, one term is always present, gameness. As previously stated, gameness is the willingness of a dog to continue fighting, or hunting, or pulling a cart, or defending his owner, through great stress, intense pain, and even until death. Gameness has nothing to do with bravery or fighting ability; it has to do with *heart*. Gameness has to do with never quitting regardless of what the opposition has put up against you.

The gameness of the APBT is awe inspiring. So game are APBTs that the United States Marine Corps adopted an APBT to be its official mascot. APBTs have been badly burned but returned to their owners' home to try to save a child. Other APBTs have struggled to save a drowning person only to die from their efforts.

Gameness in the extreme is a trait long since deemphasized in traditional dog-breeding efforts. Gameness, as the primary characteristic of a breed, is not at a premium in hunt-

ing dogs, hounds, and show dogs, or even in terriers; many other breeds can be quite determined, as with sled dogs giving their all to pull a sled in a race, but the only dog whose life regularly depended on being absolutely and totally game was the pit dog from which the APBT descended.

The need to test gameness and the desire to only possess truly game dogs may be the primary reason that dogfighting, even with severe penalties to the owners, continues to this very day. Traditional dogfighters valued gameness above all other qualities. Without gameness, a dog under the stress of the pit would quit. Quitting was (and is) the worst imaginable sin to a dogfighter. An APBT may be soundly beaten in the pit, but if he is game and keeps on keeping on until the match is over, the dog is still a solid success in the eyes of his owner and most of the spectators.

One reason that APBT fans are so united in their insistence that the American Staffordshire is a different breed, even though it sprang from the same canine gene pool, is that most APBT fans who value gameness no longer consider the Amstaff to be game. This doesn't bother most Amstaff people, but it is one true dividing line between the two camps. The game-bred advocates won't even breed their game-bred APBTs to other APBTs that may not be game bred, much less an Amstaff. From the perspective of gameness, the APBT and the Amstaff are as far from being the same breed as the Collie and the Border Collie are in sheepherding ability.

Power and Strength

Strength is one of the defining characteristics of the APBT. Strength can legitimately be thought of as stored energy in reserve; power is energy in actual use. Breed fans are fond of bragging that a 40-pound (18 kg) APBT is as powerful as any other dog in the world at twice the size. Power for an APBT is a by-product of over 150 years of having to be strong enough to survive in the direst of circumstances. The APBT not only survived the decades of pit fighting, but he thrived in the process. The remaining dogs were strong and capable of taking on any task, or any opponent.

The APBT possesses an incredible amount of strength. If power is the amount of force a dog can deliver in a concerted manner, strength is the source of that power. American Pit Bull Terriers have excelled at the growing sport of weight pulling by moving more weight than any other breed near their size. What once aided in the wrestling phase of dogfighting now gives the breed the capacity to be very strong dogs in very small packages.

To understand APBTs, one must understand the power and strength of APBTs that have never been fighting dogs. Gaining control of this power and strength is the only way you can come to feel comfortable in owning dogs of this breed. Gameness is the ability to go on and on regardless of distractions and hurdles of pain and discomfort. When such a game dog is also extremely powerful and strong, great responsibility falls on this dog's owner.

One dog breeder referred to this triumvirate of gameness/power/strength as the automotive equivalent of a "small car with a huge motor, a quick response transmission, minimal brakes, and a virtually unlimited gas tank." The driver of such a car must be alert and in control at all times to avoid accidents and possible carnage. This driver's skills and reflexes should be above average.

Aggressiveness Toward Other Dogs

Many breeds of dogs are animal-aggressive to one degree or another. The popular Jack Russell Terrier, often animal-aggressive, as other members of the terrier group usually are, was originally bred to do battle with rats, badgers, foxes, and other animals. Jack Russells were bred to help deplete the huge number of rats in the days before other reliable extermination processes. To expect the average JRT not to go after a stray cat or trespassing dog is to be unrealistic, but that is not to say that dogs can't be trained and socialized to ignore other animals. This is possible with the Jack Russell and it is possible with the APBT. Dogs that grow up with other animals generally reach an accommodation of their own.

It is important to recognize that APBTs and Tosa Inus, as fighting breeds, don't respond to challenges in the same way that nonfighting breeds do. Most dogs are merely trying to establish dominance over their opponent. When that opponent gives in and strikes classical submission positions, cowering or rolling over onto its back, most dominant dogs are satisfied and the fight stops.

Game-Bred Dogs

When game-bred dogs confront each other, neither of them will submit to the other. Gameness requires that they never give up. When a fight begins between two game dogs, whether either has ever been in a pit before or not, the fight will not stop unless death or human beings stop it. Gameness brings a whole new dimension to a dogfight. No bristling and dominance displays here. There is very little time for a human to intervene after the aggressiveness starts. This is no contest to see

who will be top dog, leader of the pack. This fight is more serious with life or death hanging in the balance,

One of the outward signs that one sees at kennels (often called "yards") where game-bred APBTs are kept is a complete separation of most adults of both sexes. APBTs are often difficult to kennel because of their strength and intense desire to get at other dogs in the area.

Some game-bred dog breeders have dogs that are perfectly safe around other dogs when out and away from the yard. One breeder, the owner of ten dogs, stated, "I have one dog that I can walk on the streets or in parks and he won't be aggressive unless another dog acts in a threatening manner." This same breeder has nine other dogs that he doesn't feel comfortable in taking out to places where they may encounter other dogs.

Positive Attributes

Lack of Aggressiveness Toward Humans

In several places in this book we have made reference to the fact that, contrary to the avalanche of public opinion, APBTs from properly bred litters with proper socialization and proper training are much less a threat to bite humans than are most other breeds of dogs and mixtures of breeds.

In the earlier discussion about dog-aggressive behavior, an APBT breeder pointed out that nine of his ten dogs weren't really safe to handle around other strange dogs. Ironically, this same breeder has had several

American Pit Bull Terriers stolen right from his backyard! Strangers have been able to walk in and unchain friendly APBTs and lead the not human-aggressive dogs away. Some APBT breeders have even gone to the expense of buying dogs of other breeds to keep around their property to serve as a guard system to protect the APBTs from being dognapped.

Loyalty

Another positive attribute that has been instilled in the APBT is incredible loyalty. Perhaps an offshoot of the well-documented gameness attribute that is legendary within this breed, loyalty in an APBT is focused and directed toward a specific aspect of a dog's life. The APBT whose ancestors fought in pits with survival as the main focus now find protecting the members of its immediate family worthy of intense concentration. Old APBT breeders are fond of saying that you and your children are never safer than when with a game-bred APBT.

Companionability

A logical attachment to gameness and loyalty is a high companionability quotient for the American Pit Bull Terrier. They are accustomed to being near their people. They really enjoy human attention and they enjoy spending time with their owners. The APBT is a strong and confident companion whose main purpose in life is to serve his master or mistress, even if it means stress, even if it means discomfort, and even if it means death.

Understanding the APBT requires acceptance of the total package. The strength and power cannot be seen clearly without acknowledging the personality and charm. The toughness of the breed cannot be fully reckoned with without assessing the gentleness of the breed. The APBT's harshly real background should not be a focal point without considering the funny, clownish antics of the dog. In understanding the complete APBT, a potential owner should take into account all facets of sharing one's life with a pet of complexity.

• The APBT can be the most complete of family dogs.
• Without proper training and socialization, an APBT can be a great liability.
• Properly housed, an APBT will be less trouble than many other breeds.

• Improperly housed and controlled, the APBT can be more trouble than you can ever imagine.
• The APBT is ready to give its life for its family.
• The APBT requires time with its family.
• The properly bred APBT can be a total joy to live with.
• The properly bred APBT will need to be protected from situations that could cause harm.
• The APBT is many times less likely to bite a human than most other breeds of dogs.
• If an APBT does bite someone, it could be much more serious than a bite from other breeds.

Before you seriously consider adding an APBT to your life, take time—a lot of time—to understand what this breed is and what it is not.

Chapter Seven

Owning an APBT

Know Thyself

Before you even consider owning an American Pit Bull Terrier, you must take a fearless and searching moral inventory of yourself and your family. No dog deserves an inadequate or incomplete owner, and this is many more times true for the APBT. Unless you and your family can live up to a fairly stiff list of qualifications, get another breed of dog—or perhaps get no dog at all. Try to answer the following questions truthfully and honestly.

• Are you willing to spend the appropriate amount of time, money, and energy finding the right APBT for you and your family?

• Are you willing to make certain that the living arrangements you plan for your APBT will be more than just adequate and will provide 100 percent for the safety and well-being of your pet?

• Do you have the self-discipline to see that your APBT is properly trained, properly socialized, and properly cared for throughout the dog's life?

• Is each member of your family fully committed to providing the care that an APBT will require?

• Are you able to resist the childish propensity to gloat about having "the toughest dog on the block?"

• Can you make absolutely certain that no one in your family will ever be tempted to let your APBT get into a fight with another dog, no matter how obnoxious that other dog may be?

• Can you handle the recriminations from the ignorant and unknowing who may assume the worst about you when they see you own a "pit bull?"

• Are you ready for the closer scrutiny that may come your way from insurance companies and from some governmental agencies?

• Can you allow an APBT to become a complete companion animal to you by becoming a complete companion human to the dog?

Know Thy Situation

The American Pit Bull Terrier is a tough and adaptable dog, but even the smartest APBT is still just a dog. Before you own an APBT, you must make sure your family situation, home environment, work schedule, circle of friends and relatives, and lifestyle are appropriate for such a dog. The APBT has great potential to be a great pet, but only in a setting that is conducive to maximizing its attributes and minimizing its negatives. Unless you can assure such a pet of a safe and loving home, then the APBT is definitely *not* the dog for you! Some questions about your personal situation should be answered prior to any serious thought about obtaining an APBT.

• Can you, and will you, allow your APBT to live inside your home with your family and you?

• Do you have room in your schedules to give an APBT some quality time several times each day?

• Do you fully realize all that is required in owning any dog, as well as what is required in owning an APBT?

• Can you constantly safeguard your APBT from getting away from your control and into harm's way?

• Does your lifestyle have enough appropriate room for an APBT? Are the things you enjoy doing going to be things in which you can safely and comfortably include your APBT?

• Does your household lend itself to the inclusion of an APBT with ample room for the dog to be comfortable and kept from dangerous or troublesome situations?

• Can you, in good conscience, honestly state that an APBT will find a good and safe home with your family?

Know the APBT

Unless you know what owning an APBT truly involves, you are setting yourself (and an innocent dog) up for what could be a failure of monumental proportions. Owning an APBT can be a wonderful experience, but never be deluded that this is just another dog. Not only is much to be gained—by the right individual or family under the right circumstances—by owning an APBT, but much is required.

In seeking to know all you can about the APBT, take the high road and learn from a wide variety of sources. You are fortunate that these sources are readily accessible (some of them are listed in Useful Addresses and Literature, page 170). A suggested course of study about the APBT would include the following:

Books, Videos, Internet

Books on the subject of dogs are easy to find at your public library, in bookstores, or through the Internet. You might want to read about the Amstaff, the Staffordshire Bull Terrier, and other related breeds. It is important to read several books written from several perspectives and not just those that discuss only a breed's good points.

There are some videos about the APBT, the American Staffordshire, the Staffordshire Bull Terrier, the Bull Terrier, the American Bulldog, and similar breeds. These are available through the specific kennel clubs and other sources.

There are a large number of sites available to those seeking information about the APBT and related breeds. The American Dog Breeders Association, the United Kennel Club, and the American Kennel Club all maintain excellent web sites. Numerous APBT clubs, rescue organizations, and concerned groups—for and against the APBT—can be contacted through the Internet. General dog organizations with widely diverse information to share also have articles to read, concerns to be shared, and chat rooms to be joined. Information about any breed and virtually any aspect of any breed is readily available if you are seriously interested in learning.

Breeders and Breed Clubs

The APBT and all of the related breeds are very willing to share information with interested individuals.

Breed Clubs (see Useful Addresses and Literature, page 170) can provide the names of approved APBT breeders in many parts of the United States. These individual breeders, though a varied lot with different goals and objectives, can tell a potential dog owner much about the breed from their own perspectives.

The breed clubs can provide prospective owners with the dates and locations of club meetings, local dog shows, obedience events, and other activities. Most clubs are genuinely interested in the betterment of their respective breeds; new members are the life's blood of such organizations. Somewhere in these clubs and associations are knowledgeable people with interests similar to those of almost any APBT-seeker.

Events

Because of the great versatility of the APBT, there are many activities that the owners of these dogs attend and in which their dogs participate. While there are still some covert (and possibly illegal) activities involving the APBT, most novices will not be invited to attend even if that was the novice's goal. There are dozens of other APBT-related events that don't stretch the limits of the law and these are usually very interesting to attend. They include:

• Conformation shows, which are those in which dogs are judged against the written standards of the various breeds. Various kennel clubs and dog registries sanction these shows and keep calendars of when

these shows are held throughout the United States. Such shows are great places to meet breeders of conformation dogs. One can also see what the APBT looks like in the flesh, the various colors, and something of the preparation and care that go into getting a show dog ready to compete.

• Obedience events, which are those in which APBTs and other breeds are able to win obedience titles (see Obedience Training, page 126) by obeying increasingly complex series of commands under a variety of circumstances. Obedience trials are also great places to make contacts with APBT owners. Such owners may also be conformation breeders or they may own just one or two dogs that they train for obedience activities only.

• Schutzhund events, which involve dogs that have been tested to show what they have learned in training for protective purposes. Some APBTs do well in this high-energy activity.

There are a number of other events that involve training dogs in certain task-oriented activities. Some of these involve quite a few APBTs; others do not. A suggestion to any person seeking to learn about the American Pit Bull Terrier is to begin with general events, such as dog shows, and then naturally gravitate toward the more specialized activities that are ongoing within the breed.

The ultimate goal any person should have in owning a dog is to gain as much information and understanding of the various aspects of the breed. Learning about the APBT can be very interesting. Individuals and families can visit a number of APBT events, read a number of books on the breed, and talk with breed experts, in person and through the Internet. Responsible questions are generally welcomed. Even if a person or a family decides that the APBT is not right for them, the learning is not lost and may lead to involvement and ownership of a related, or completely different, breed or type of dog.

Is the APBT Right for You?

The harvest of your efforts in learning about the APBT will be reaped in how you answer this question. You may have concluded that the APBT is an excellent dog with a number of wonderful attributes and that it is exactly the perfect dog—for someone else! Or, you may have decided that you like what you hear about the APBT and are ready to pursue the possibility of adopting such a dog into your home. You may have decided that

the breed remains somewhat of a mystery to you and you need more time. You may have decided to look at another breed or perhaps no breed at all, but just a mixed-breed dog. If you have arrived at any of these positions without impulsively deluding yourself, then you are to be congratulated! It is far better to carefully study this breed and then decide *not* to get an APBT than it is to become captivated by the supposed allure of the former pit breed and make an unwise decision.

Many experienced dog people can look at the needs of the APBT as they fit into your lifestyle and give you a reasonably accurate assessment about the rightness of the APBT for you. You are the only person who can accept or reject such information. You need to make this decision based on truth. Your decision about whether the APBT is right for you should *not* be based on public misperceptions about the breed, media hype about the breed, any need to enhance your concept of yourself by owning a dog with a macho image, the idea that you can raise a few pit bulls and make some money in the process, a skewed view about the APBT as the ultimate protection dog, which it is not, the desire to walk on the wild or dark side of dog owning, the view that an APBT will be a nice fashion accessory for you to sport about town.

Your decision about whether the APBT is right for you *should* be based on a realistic look at the good and bad aspects of this breed after a detailed quest for unbiased information about the breed, what you have seen, with your own eyes, about the breed, and how it appeals to you, a factual assessment of the laws and regulations, including those involving insurance, that apply where you live, the amount of time you will be able to spend helping to develop your APBT into a first-class companion animal, and your desire to be a responsible APBT owner with appropriate consideration of the rights and feelings of those around you.

Are You Right for the APBT?

Certainly as important as your attitude about whether the APBT is right for you is your assessment of whether you are right for the APBT. In some aspects, this is an even harder evaluation to make, but it must be done and it must be done accurately. Conscientiously answering the following questions, and

others of your own, can help in this self-assessment process.

• Do you have sufficient experience with other dogs so that you aren't going into APBT ownership as a complete novice?

• Have you taken sufficient time to learn about the breed?

• Do you have enough money to obtain the best APBT that meets your requirements—a quality APBT puppy may cost over $500, with top-quality dogs costing much more—and then to properly contain, house, care for, and train such a dog?

• Do the other members of your household share your attitude about the APBT?

• Does your lifestyle allow you to spend daily time with your APBT?

• Does the idea of being seen walking with a powerful, impressive-looking APBT give you an ego boost or a thrill of anticipation?

• Are you fully cognizant of the dog laws, regulations, and restrictions in your area of residence?

• Do you want to own an APBT for what the dog can do for you, what you can do for the dog, or what you can do for each other?

• Are matters in your marriage and personal life stable enough to bring another living creature to share your life?

Your answers to these and other questions will really determine your suitability to own an APBT. If you have answered these and other self-searching inquiries honestly,

you now have a good idea about whether you are right for the APBT.

The APBT has much to offer the right owner. The right owner will have to be responsible for ownership of such a complex dog. Most long-time owners of the APBT readily admit that some parts of ownership of this breed are quite challenging, but that for every second of challenge the dog brings, it also brings dozens of wonderful hours and a huge amount of love and loyalty to its human owners.

Understanding the APBT, perhaps more than any other breed of dog, requires an understanding of your own personal motivations and those of your family. Without the latter, you can never have the former.

Special Concerns for APBT Owners

Insurance Companies and the APBT

Most homeowners' insurance policies cover dog bites. This coverage includes cases where your pet bites someone, there are medical expenses, and this individual decides to sue you. The amount of coverage, however, is based on the limits of your homeowner's policy. Insurance underwriters are showing more and more concern if you own an APBT or other large and potentially aggressive dog. Insurers now pay many hundreds of millions of dollars each year to settle dog bite claims.

One insurance expert who admires the APBT warns dog owners against not having enough coverage. Owners of APBTs and other breeds are faced with a sad inevitability—own an APBT, pay higher insurance costs.

Our Litigious Society

More and more owners of American Pit Bull Terriers are practicing "risk management" regarding their dogs. Some people have not replaced their APBTs after their pet's death. Others are moving to rural areas where the likelihood of contact with a litigious person is smaller. Still others are living their entire lives with a paranoia that almost knows no bounds.

Responsible dog owners who take regular care will avoid most legal problems. Socialization (see page 85) and training (see page 107) will overcome most of the negatives. In one case, when it was claimed that a suspicious-looking wound was a dog bite from an aging APBT, the dog owner's attorney measured the bite radius of the alleged APBT attacker and found that the size of the mouth of the dog could not possibly have made the wound. Later, a veterinarian testified that the old dog didn't have enough teeth to do that much damage!

Responsible pet owners, especially responsible owners of APBTs, will practice risk management to avoid becoming embroiled in problems that eventually become lawsuits. Strong gates, doors that are secure, and a family that is alert to the needs (and safety) of its pet will go a long way toward keeping the APBT at home and out of court. To head off litigation before it happens, be aware of the following points.

• Socialize, socialize, and socialize.

• If your pet is aggressive toward other dogs, stay away from an area where other dogs are roaming unattended.

• Always assume a problem can occur and be prepared to prevent it.

• Do a daily check on the equipment and control items you depend on to keep your APBT out of trouble, such

as fences, entry doors, collars and leads, and others.

• Carry a muzzle with you when you are out walking with your APBT.

• Don't brag about owning a "pit bull" or an APBT.

• Keep training current for you and your dog.

Breed-specific Legislation

More of a threat to the APBT, and many other fine breeds, are those who would legislate the APBT out of existence. Certainly there are legitimate protections that all citizens deserve and should demand. One of these is freedom from the depredations and nuisances of vicious and out-of-control pets. If a person owns any kind of animal and that animal poses a threat to the general good and general population, action is warranted.

Just because a dog of a particular breed, or a particular breed type, is vicious does not mean that any other members of that same breed will act in the same manner. Certainly "shotgun"-approach legislation violates more than the rights of a dog; such broad-brush prohibitions run counter to the foundations of freedom on which the United States was founded.

We are indeed a country of laws, but we are not automatically a country of lawbreakers. Dogs that have been caught in the gill net legislative approach that does away with entire breeds of dogs and not with specific wrongdoers is not in keeping with individual rights. All citizens

of conscience deplore dog bites and dog attacks on children and other innocent individuals. To automatically ban all dogs because of the actions of a few or even only one dog smacks of something that deeply threatens the foundations of our freedoms. The guarantee of due process under the law and other Constitutional safeguards were designed to prevent an erosion of individual rights while protecting the rights of the general public.

Breed-specific laws appear to be a "quick fix" to the escalating problem of dog bites, but most of these regulatory "silver bullets" miss the fact that *individual* dogs bite, not entire breeds and classes of dogs. In Europe there is a group of extremists whose stated mission is to eliminate all breeds of dogs that don't fall within a narrowly defined vision of what dogs ought to look like. All the giant breeds—Great Danes, Saint Bernards, Mastiffs, and others—would no longer be allowed. All long-bodied, short-legged dogs—Bassets, Corgis, Scotties, and others—would be neutered and disappear after this generation. All toy dog breeds—Yorkshire Terriers, Chihuahuas, Pomeranians—would also be forever banned. Extremely longhaired breeds such as the Old English Sheepdog, the Puli, the Keeshond, and others would no longer exist. Short-faced dogs such as the Bulldog, the Boston Terrier, and the French Bulldog would become extinct.

The goal of this group is to have dogs without all the physical abnor-

"Peterrorists"

There are individuals and organizations that consider the ownership of a pet to be akin to involuntary servitude. Some of these people have targeted APBTs and their owners in efforts that could see your pet "freed from the prison of its backyard and allowed to run free." Other people will steal an APBT for any of a variety of reasons; perhaps some of them are street criminals that have done so much harm to the APBT's reputation with their street pit dogs. In any case, your APBT will be in a bad way. However unlikely, a number of dog owners have experienced difficulties brought on by others with strange and illegal agendas. There are some ways that responsible dog breeders can protect themselves and their dogs from any threat, real or imagined. Most law enforcement people would recommend some of these steps, even if you are not the owner of an APBT.

• Keep your APBT with you as an in-home pet as much as possible.

• Be suspicious of strangers who see you with your dog and come over to chat. If you don't know these people, don't answer questions about your dog and yourself.

• Take a small camera with you when you are out on walks with your dog, and take pictures of any suspicious-looking people.

• Have a quality security system installed and use it.

• Have your APBT photographed, tattooed, and microchipped for identification purposes.

• Because you have an even-tempered family dog and are not involved in any illegal activity, you and your APBT should make friends with the law enforcement people in your neighborhood.

malities, size differences, and other factors that cost pet owners so much every year. The giant breeds all have short life spans; the short-legged and long-bodied dogs often have very serious back problems. Toy breeds are obviously unnatural (according to this European group) and they have many medical problems. Longhaired breeds have coats that are easily matted and hide a multitude of health problems. The brachycephalic dogs have breathing problems.

This organization really exists and their goals are accurately portrayed. Their mission is to return dogs to a norm that would be considered healthy, with no exaggerated physical features, medium-sized, with short hair. Ironically, the dog this group seems to be advocating sounds a lot like the APBT!

Chapter Eight
Living with an APBT

There are all kinds of dog owners and all kinds of living situations regarding dogs and their owners. A dog like the APBT is tough enough and adaptable enough to survive just about anything, but really shouldn't have to. Some game-bred APBT owners say that because this breed has often been kept chained for over 100 years, it is not stressed by such an existence as other breeds would be.

There may be no studies available to prove or disprove this assertion, but many breeds do much better the more time they spend with their owners. This is true for the American Pit Bull Terrier, a breed that loves the attention and affection of being near its family.

The Right Attitude

Public perceptions about the APBT run so strongly in some locales that an APBT running free is, in some minds, a major threat to the safety and tranquility of the community. Unfortunately, some law enforcement organizations have the same kind of fear about the APBT

and may act or react accordingly. If your Beagle or Collie or other breed, or mixture of breeds, gets out of its backyard, the community response is to help save the escaped pet from being killed in traffic. For an APBT, or even a dog that just resembles an APBT, the focus suddenly shifts away from the dog's safety toward the community's safety.

To keep a pet APBT out of harm's way is to be doubly or triply certain that the dog is under control at all times. Control may be expressed in the form of a strong collar and leash firmly held by you, or an inside crate where the APBT can rest and relax when you and your family are not at home for brief periods of time. Control could be a strong, tall, escape-proof backyard fence or kennel.

The right attitude about owning an APBT is taught to the children in the home. Lessons about being certain that the family pet doesn't slip through an open door or open gate should be taught early. Children should be impressed with the importance of keeping their pet away from strange dogs. They should also be impressed with the notion that the family dog must

always be considered when there are family activities. Keeping your American Pit Bull Terrier safe becomes an entire family goal.

The Right Environment

An environment, that keeps the family APBT out of dangerous situations is essential. As stated, your pet must be kept under control at all times. This does not mean perpetual imprisonment, house arrest, or exile to the kennel in the backyard. It does mean that the dog is never allowed to run free in the neighborhood, and that only older, respon-

sible children are allowed to walk your APBT without parental supervision. It does mean that family friends are asked not to bring their pets with them when they visit, unless your dog was thoroughly socialized with these same pets as a puppy.

The right environment for an APBT is a house or an apartment where the dog is kept comfortable and safe from any outside interactions that could result in serious problems. The ideal home should have an area where the dog's crate would be out of drafts and direct sun. Your APBT should have access to the crate so the dog can take a break from the hectic life of being a dog.

Your American Pit Bull Terrier's outside kennel should be securely

placed into the ground to prevent the dog from digging out. The kennel should be covered to make climbing out impossible.

Under most circumstances, it is recommended that the APBT be primarily, if not exclusively, an inside dog. His short coat and medium size make him a good inside pet. Taking your APBT out for walks and relief breaks will make the dog a better pet while avoiding outside kennels.

Setting the Stage for Success

There are some ways that a family or an individual can prepare for, and ensure, success for an APBT as a companion animal. Success is

defined as giving the pet the opportunity to reach his potential while keeping him protected from conditions and circumstances that are far from safe. You should always be alert to potential hazards.

Properly socializing an APBT puppy will help that puppy recognize that other dogs, people, and situations usually pose no threat. It is important to provide a young puppy, in its formative stages, with a large number of positive experiences. A well-socialized dog, of any breed, is more adaptable to changing circumstances later in life. This need for adaptability is much more important in an APBT than in most other breeds and kinds of dogs.

If each member of the family is truly concerned about the well-being of the pet, success is greatly enhanced. If the dangers of your American Pit Bull Terrier being left alone on the street are clearly faced and discussed, every person in the home can pay extra attention to be sure that the dog stays at home or under human control when the dog does leave the confines of the household.

Setting the Stage for Failure

Failure, like success, can be orchestrated. If a home is unprepared for the arrival of an APBT, failure starts right there. If the APBT is perceived to be just another dog without appropriate safeguards built in for the benefit of the pet, the chance of failure increases. With an insecure and poorly socialized APBT in a careless and neglectful environment, the potential for a negative incident becomes much more likely.

When a family or an individual provides little or no consistent care for a dog, that dog lives a miserable existence. An APBT in such a setting can easily become troublesome to itself and to other pets in the neighborhood. Impulsively buying an APBT with little or no awareness of the positives and not-so-positives about the breed can, in today's litigious society, economically devastate an individual or a family. An undisciplined APBT running free and uncontrolled in the climate of distrust and fear that already exists about this breed is an ambulance chaser's dream.

Dealing with Negative Public Perceptions

Owning an APBT could subject a person or family to some high levels of anti-APBT sentiment. Most of these negative attitudes are based on ignorance and on the hysteria that has affected the breed for a number of years. Some very good APBTs wind up in animal shelters when their owners encounter intense public hostility about their pets. People have a right to be afraid and they also have a right to express themselves, and most APBT owners—though they may be owners of innocent dogs—have to listen to all the diatribes and barbs hurled their way about their dog.

Amazing APBTs

You have plenty of positive ammunition if you are politely accosted about why you would own such a "terrible" dog. APBTs have done some amazing things, such as "Weela," who won the 1993 Ken-L-Ration Dog Hero of the Year by performing bravely during severe flooding in Texas. (Weela was one of a litter of five four-week-old APBT puppies abandoned and left to die before the Watkins family saved them, adopted out the other littermates, and kept Weela as their family pet). Stubby, who the AKC consistently referred to as a "mongrel" and still does to this day, was an APBT who became the most decorated canine in World War I. Lucenay's Peter, better known as "Petey," was the canine supporting actor who worked with "Spanky" and "Alfalfa" in the 1930s *Our Gang* series that starred the Little Rascals. Petey, also known as "Pete the Pup," was among the first APBTs to be registered by the newly formed United Kennel Club. Petey led a double life; he was also one of the first American Staffordshire Terriers registered in the American Kennel Club.

How do you handle these comments? Develop a thick skin, realizing that the critics don't know your dog and don't know the breed in general. Ignore such caustic remarks and never indulge in harsh words of your own. Certainly never become threatening or allow yourself to be pulled into a physical altercation. This only reinforces what the attackers believe and have been saying. The most foolish and detrimental thing you could do would be to, even in jest, set your APBT on any of the detractors!

The best way to overcome such adversity is to do everything possible to make certain that there is no validity in any of the unflattering things said about your dog. This approach calls for socialization, training, and appropriate behavior whenever you and your APBT are in the public eye. If your pet is a show champion, an obedience title holder, certified as a therapy dog, or has attained some other positive achievement, make sure it gets in the newspaper or becomes a topic of neighborhood conversation.

When ill-informed bullies want to classify every APBT owner as a dog-fighter or some sort of latent criminal, you can gently remind them of some other APBT owners who kept one step ahead of the law: Helen Keller owned an APBT, writer James Thurber owned one and wrote about it, President Theodore Roosevelt owned an APBT and praised the dog to his friends, Thomas Edison was a fan of the APBT, as was the Shakespearean actor-turned-beloved United States senator, Everett McKinley Dirksen. Jack Dempsey, John L. Sullivan, Jack Johnson—all heavyweight champs—owned APBTs.

Many thousands of people have owned APBTs and have never had any problems or incidents concerning their dogs. The attacks attributed to APBTs, as terrible as these attacks are, have been perpetrated by the tiniest of minorities of an extremely popular breed. Not many breeds in the English Kennel Club, the American Kennel Club, or the United Kennel Club can face the intense scrutiny that the APBT has had to encounter. Many breeds have a far worse track record of biting people than does the American Pit Bull Terrier, even with the heightened publicity and constant scrutiny that the APBT receives.

Commonsense Precautions

There is no need to live in constant fear of your APBT becoming involved in a dog bite case and you and your family becoming embroiled in a sticky legal battle. While such things do happen, they are extremely rare; if you and your family use common sense, they will be rarer still.

• When out with your dog in public, always keep your APBT under control.

• Be ever alert that while you may be sure of *your* dog, other dogs in public parks, on city streets, and elsewhere may attempt to initiate some physical altercation.

• Be aware that some people will steal APBTs right out of your yard, and that some APBTs will let them.

• For safety purposes treat your APBT like a precocious toddler and keep doors closed, gates locked, and other hazards fenced away.

• Socialize your APBT puppy (see page 85) until it has met many kinds of people, seen every kind of potentially scary thing, such as bicycles and wheelchairs, and met other friendly animals.

• Avoid places where dogs are allowed to run free.

• Remember that no matter how good a dog your American Pit Bull Terrier may be, he is still just a dog that needs your protection.

For more on the public and the APBT, see page 90.

Chapter Nine

The APBT as a Pet and Companion

Socialization

The need for good socialization of your APBT is stressed throughout this book. Perhaps more than any other single issue, other than maintaining control of your APBT, socialization is the most important.

There is a crucial window of time and opportunity in a puppy's life that allows bonding with human beings. Usually in the first few weeks of life, this window gives a trusting puppy the chance to learn to trust humans. After this time has passed, most dogs never completely trust people, and while they may be tamed to some extent, their opportunity to become real companion animals has generally gone forever.

Socialization is facilitated by introducing a puppy to a variety of people and experiences in a controlled environment to set the boundaries of trust and interaction for the pup's later life. Socialization is providing experiences where a puppy isn't frightened. This process is best undertaken in a carefully organized manner. It involves taking a puppy to places that are different from any that it has encountered so far in its brief life, as well as meeting different people.

There is some danger in socialization, and this must be countered by good judgment and care on a puppy owner's part. Puppies that have not had their complete round of vaccinations are susceptible to a number of diseases. To avoid exposure to these diseases, puppies younger than eight weeks that have not had their first shots should be kept at home, with socialization occurring within the family only.

Novice puppy owners should have their veterinarian's approval prior to taking a puppy to locations where many dogs and people that have been around dogs are present. The following is a sample plan to fully socialize an APBT puppy that has had its basic immunizations.

1. After you have owned your pup for several weeks and it feels comfortable with you, a visit to the kennel where he was born might be arranged. This provides a blending of his fast-fading previous life and his current life with you.

2. Since you will want to be able to take your American Pit Bull Terrier out with you in public, plan on giving your pet an opportunity to meet and positively interact with people of other races, genders, and appearances than yourself.

3. If you are a female and there are no adult males living in your household, be certain that you stage puppy socialization interaction with a number of adult males in and out of your home.

4. If you are of a particular ethnic group, allow your pup to be positively socialized by people of other ethnic backgrounds.

5. If there are no children in your home, allow children of several age groups, and under careful adult supervision, to play with your APBT puppy. Be careful that a very young child doesn't accidentally hurt the puppy or cause him to feel uncomfortable.

6. Go to parks and pet products stores that welcome well-behaved dogs. Let your puppy be around the people and other pets in this public location, avoiding any negative experiences for the impressionable youngster.

7. Introduce your puppy to people of all ages and physical descriptions; be sure to include people in wheelchairs and those who use canes and walkers.

8. Let your APBT pup observe people riding on motorcycles, bicycles, horseback, rollerblading, or skateboarding. Other dogs, under the control of their owners, can be introduced to your puppy, but avoid any rough play that might trigger aggressive responses.

9. If you want your APBT to be well behaved, don't engage in rough play with the dog. Many American Pit Bull Terriers have been trained to chew on tire swings and other objects; as a pet owner, you would be wise to avoid ever playing tug-of-war with your dog. Why get into a contest with your pet that it might misunderstand?

10. Never let your APBT fight or even mock-fight with other dogs. If fighting isn't started, it may not immediately occur as the pup's only appropriate response as it gets older.

11. If you are going to be in an urban setting with your APBT, be certain to acquaint the pup with walking in crowds and riding on elevators and escalators, and get him used to traffic noises.

12. If you live in a rural setting where your APBT might be confronted by farm animals, be certain to take the young dog around such creatures as early and as often as possible.

13. If you choose to enter certain dog-related events and activities with your APBT, take the growing puppy to dog shows, obedience trials, Schutzhund events, agility contests, weight pulls, or any other activities to familiarize the pup with them.

14. If you have frequent houseguests, always take time to socialize your APBT with them. Explain to the humans about the rules concerning preventing the dog from getting through an open door or gate.

15. Continue socialization as often as possible throughout the dog's life, but socialization must be started early to be effective.

Children and the APBT

Before the years of the public fear and hostility toward the breed, the American Pit Bull Terrier was considered an excellent companion for children. One of the reasons that producer/director Hal Roach of *Little Rascals* and *Our Gang* fame chose Petey over Rin-Tin-Tin and Lassie to be the children's companion was his acknowledged affinity for and connection with children. The true APBT still has a great love for children.

As with all dogs, very small children need to be supervised by adults any time they are with an APBT. This precaution is not so much for the children as it is for the APBT. Eye gouging, ear twisting, and tail biting or pulling may not severely injure an adult dog, but a puppy could be hurt and come to fear children.

If a computer were given unbiased information about dogs and children, and given the directive to design a perfect canine pet for children, it is quite possible that the APBT would mirror the computer design. Medium-sized, shorthaired, clownish personality, ability to play all day long with the most rambunctious children, and a great lover of youngsters, the APBT has many of the desired characteristics.

The true American Pit Bull Terrier has always, even in old pit dog days, been a family pet. Many pit dogs were taken back home after a fight. They returned to their role as a child's companion, a stock dog, and family pet. The APBT would not have survived as a breed or have achieved the high levels of popularity that it did if it was a danger to children.

Other Pets and the APBT

Regardless of the view of some APBT fans, the word "terrier" still appears in the breed's name. History records that the APBT descended in part from terrier breeds. There is no

legitimate evidence to the contrary, so the APBT is probably at least part terrier. As such, terriers were bred to be killers of rats, foxes, badgers, and the like. Most terriers cannot be trusted with small animals. Care must be taken with all terrier breeds around other pets.

APBTs that have been raised from their early puppy years with other kinds of pets are generally much safer around different animals as they grow older. Any terrier breed and most other dogs can revert to type and could do harm. Be safe rather than sorry with all dogs.

The APBT has been extensively used as a "catch" dog to help capture semiwild cattle and swine. Other APBTs have been bred for pit fighting. While many dogs of this breed can become safe around any animals, even other dogs, they must be trained and socialized. When in doubt about an APBT's behavior around other animals, always supervise the dog or keep him safely away from livestock and other pets.

Other Dogs and the APBT

The subject of how the APBT interacts with other dogs has been addressed several times because of its extreme importance. It is safer to err on the side of caution while not maligning a great dog breed. Most APBTs can be socialized and trained to leave other dogs alone. Some

APBTs can get along well with dogs of the same gender, which is usually more difficult to accomplish than with dogs of the opposite sex. This will not happen accidentally. APBTs—and many other breeds—have to be thoroughly socialized and then trained to behave around other adult dogs. Some dogs never learn to do this; some of those dogs are American Pit Bull Terriers.

All APBTs must be under the control of their owners at *all* times. This is especially true for APBTs and strange dogs. Dogs generally try to stake out new turf by threatening and intimidating potential or actual rivals for that turf. In most cases, one or the other of the dogs gives up and a battle is avoided. The APBT was bred for centuries not to give up. Threats and attempts at intimidation from another dog don't work with the APBT.

Because of the potential for conflict with strange dogs, some municipalities demand that all American Pit Bull Terriers be muzzled when out in public. While this assumes that all dogs of this breed are vicious and uncontrollable, it is better than the bans that other locales have enacted on several of the bull-and-terrier breeds.

Common sense and alertness can help keep an APBT out of trouble with other dogs. These two elements must come from the dog's owner. And remember the following.

• Never let your APBT run off leash anywhere but in his own fenced backyard.

• Assume that trouble can happen each time you and your APBT go out in public; be ready to head it off or to prevent it.
• Avoid places where there may be uncontrolled dogs.
• Even though your APBT is not aggressive, keep the dog on a strong leash with a strong collar and *always* have a muzzle with you, just in case.

The APBT as a Guard Dog

One of the great ironies of the dog world, especially considering the pit bull myths that have sprung up, is that one of the dog breeds most likely to be stolen is the APBT. As has been mentioned, even game-bred dogs that may have been used for illegal activities are very amiable and will go with strangers. If a strange dog approached these game-bred dogs, there would be quite a different outcome.

The true American Pit Bull Terrier—not "pit bulls" or imposters—has always been bred not to attack humans. This continues to be the case with an overwhelming majority of dogs of this breed. It is for this reason that a person who knows the APBT, and has not fallen prey to all the media hype and false rhetoric about the breed, could come into the home of an APBT and take out everything of value including the APBT!

Another irony about game-bred APBT kennels is that many owners of these kennels are buying dogs of other breeds: German Shepherd Dogs, Rottweillers, and others that are human-aggressive *to guard their APBTs*. Not all APBTs are such softies in the guard dog role, but many are. This is another proof positive that many of the negatives that have been said about the breed have been wrong.

That the APBT is not usually human-aggressive does not mean that you and your children are not in safe paws when an APBT is around. An APBT that might gladly leave home with a friendly stranger can become a true devil-dog if someone threatens or attacks its human family. A provoked attack changes the dog into the companion animal that many dogs of many breeds become under similar circumstances. The difference is that your Pomeranian charging to your defense is quite a different matter from your APBT doing the same thing.

Some people bring out bad behavior in some dogs. As with other dogs and the APBT, always use common sense to forestall any unwarranted aggressiveness toward any human beings. Here is another place where socialization is so important. If an APBT has been exposed to postal workers, for example, and finds them to be harmless, then postal workers have nothing to fear from the dog later in life.

The Public and the APBT

Public reaction to the American Pit Bull Terrier has already been amply documented, but dealing with

When Out and About

The following are ways to effect a positive public interaction for your APBT.
• Be presentable.
• Always have a sturdy, clean leash and collar on the dog.
• Don't fool around, even among friends, by suggesting, or even pretending, to sic your dog on someone.
• Obey public laws, park rules, and good dog owner etiquette; this means picking up after your pet.
• Be respectful of other people's feelings, even if they appear not to like your dog; the park or sidewalk is theirs too.
• If an aggressive-looking dog approaches you (on or off leash), avoid any contact if at all possible.
• Regardless of what may be said to you in a negative way, walk away and ignore a person who may have an agenda that you may not be aware of.
• If a small child wants to run up and pet your dog, advise the child to wait and approach only if you think it's safe and you can make sure that your dog won't appear to be menacing.
• Allow children to approach only if their parents approve, and then don't let an exuberant APBT accidentally bump and knock one of them down or inadvertently scratch one with an errant toenail.

an unknowing and sometimes hostile population is very important.

Public reactions to your APBT will range from delight to abhorrence, from curiosity to abject terror. If you have done your job and have developed a well-socialized, well-behaved, and well-trained APBT, you can do some good public relations work for the entire breed. If you have poorly prepared your APBT for being out in public, you can confirm the worst fears of the dog haters you encounter. Never assume that a stranger will immediately recognize that your dog is a one-in-a-million companion animal. The stranger may see only a "pit bull" on a leash held by an obvious fool. Your behavior and the behavior of your dog may be the only opportunity this stranger will ever have to see the positive side of what has become the most maligned breed in the history of dogdom. One petite female APBT owner has had several instances where she has had her dog on a secure leash and strange men have come up to her and asked if she needs to be rescued from her own dog.

Chapter Ten

Caring for Your APBT

Your APBT should always be viewed as a work in progress. As with other dogs, there will probably never come a day when you can sit back and breathe a sigh of relief that you and your APBT have finally arrived. There are no commencement exercises—except in obedience school—for most APBT owners.

Just about the time you get your American Pit Bull Terrier through puppyhood, it goes charging into that gawky period, adolescence. The adorable puppy that will become the stately adult must first go through the awkwardness of this in-between period.

One day, your APBT adult will suddenly become as comfortable as an old bedroom slipper, and you and your pet will have achieved all the goals you have set with each other. And one day, when your APBT has finally reached its prime, old age will come rolling in. This is not a quiet and gradual maturational process: One day your dog looks powerful and invincible, and the next day his muzzle is gray and his step is a little slower and his need to sleep by your chair is a little more compelling.

Your APBT as a Puppy

Most breed authorities believe that your first American Pit Bull Terrier should be a puppy and probably a female puppy. Puppies can be molded by knowledgeable owners into good companion animals. While some males and some adult APBTs also make excellent pets, females are somewhat easier to handle, and a puppy gives the average first-time APBT owner a better opportunity to be ready for the time when the dog is an adult.

Puppies require a great deal of care. This care must be consistent, understood, and supported by all members of the new puppy's home. If one person in the home does all the right things in caring for the puppy, and no one else does, that puppy will not achieve his potential as the companion animal he could have become. Providing an APBT with the things he needs is one place where all members of a household must be on the same page.

Puppies need to be crate-trained (see Crate-Training, page 111). This is a great way to make housetraining easier. One of the key aspects of crate-training is to have the crate be the place in which the puppy sleeps. For the first few days in his new home, a lonesome puppy may whine and cry. If you give in to this sad APBT puppy now, you will be reinforcing the idea that whining and crying is an appropriate response to having to stay in his crate at night. If such behavior works in this instance, a bright APBT may think that the same behavior will work anytime he is required to do something that he doesn't want to do. In the case of crate-training, everyone in the home must not give in to the wails of a puppy when doing so will teach a bad lesson.

Before your home is ready for an APBT puppy, you must carefully go over every square inch where the puppy is allowed to go: house, garage, or backyard, searching for anything that could hurt your young APBT. Here are some potential hazards:

• A puppy could chew exposed electrical wiring.

• House- and yard plants may be poisonous and could kill a still-gnawing puppy.

• A puppy could swallow tacks, pins, needles, and other tiny items.

• A puppy could wedge his way between the rails on a deck or second-story landing and fall to his death.

• Chemicals, cleaners, and antifreeze can put an end to a pup's life if swallowed.

• Sharp objects, even sharp leaves on plants, could cause blindness in a young dog when accidentally poked into his eyes.

• Doors that can be nudged open by an inquisitive puppy could lead to a dangerous outside escape.

• Access to the garage could expose a puppy to lubricant leaks or put him under the tires of the family car.

• Tight places behind appliances, upright pianos, and other furniture could trap a puppy that might injure himself while trying to escape.

• Leashes and collars, especially training collars, left on an unsupervised puppy (or dog) could become snagged and the animal could be strangled.

• Heavy objects on insecure shelves or tables could fall or be pulled off by a playful puppy and crush the youngster.

• Steep stairs could be a place of danger for a young pup.

• Young puppies could drown in hot tubs, swimming pools, children's wading pools, and even koi and goldfish ponds.

• A puppy's head could get caught in the opening in some fences.

• Family activities need to be monitored because a young dog could be hurt by a hard-hit baseball or a missed basketball shot.

• Even clothes in a closet can pose potential danger to a very young puppy that could pull down some heavy winter garments upon himself and smother under the pile.

• Insecticides in and around the house and cleaning-fluid fumes on furniture and draperies could make a young pup quite ill.

• Chocolate and alcohol are toxic to dogs.

• Keep young pups off the furniture; falls or jumps off furniture could hurt a young dog.

Your APBT puppy needs to have a close and long-lasting relationship with your veterinarian. Only by becoming a regular visitor to the animal clinic can your dog avoid the many illnesses and pitfalls that lurk out in the real world. In the chapter on health care (see page 143), you will find further information about immunizations, dealing with internal and external parasites, and how to prevent health problems before they arise. Your APBT will benefit from socialization and training and you will gain the kind of pet you wanted all along if you conscientiously work on these two important areas.

In deciding to bring an American Pit Bull Terrier puppy into your home, you have embarked on a journey that will bring you to new challenges and issues. You must learn how to shape this young and impressionable puppy. Whatever this youngster becomes—good or bad—will largely depend on you. If the job doesn't seem important to you, remember that your small ten-week-old puppy will grow into a powerful adult APBT in an incredibly short time. That will happen whether you are serious and work hard with your puppy or if you are neglectful and lazy. Either way, in only a matter of months you will have an adult APBT on your hands and the time for socialization will be largely past. The best time for training will be long gone and the time for instilling early lessons will be over.

Spaying and Neutering

While your APBT is still young, you have a very important issue to resolve. That issue involves having your APBT spayed if she is a female and neutered if he is a male. Perhaps one dog in a thousand is truly of sufficient quality to be used as breeding stock. Breeding APBTs is much tougher, if you really have the good of the breed in mind, than simply owning one. There is only one legitimate reason to enter into dog breeding: the improvement of the breed. There are plenty of top-quality APBTs out there to handle that chore. One of the biggest problems facing these dogs is a population explosion among poorly bred dogs that are falsely identified as members of this grand, old breed.

Don't become part of the problem so that your children can see the "miracle of birth." Get them a video on that subject designed for children. Don't breed your APBT just so you can have one of your beloved dog's puppies. Don't get talked into breeding your dog with your neighbor's pit bull so you can get some of your money back by selling puppies. Don't let your brother-in-law fix up your dog with a blind date with a Mastiff, an American Bulldog, or a Chihuahua "just to see what the pups will look like."

If you have followed the advice given earlier and have purchased a female puppy, she can be spayed within her first six months of life. You will never have to worry about her coming into season, about male dogs coming to call, or about the risk of an unwanted litter. If she is spayed (has an ovariohysterectomy) prior to her first heat, most reputable authorities believe that she will avoid a number of health problems that consistently plague females that haven't been spayed, such as certain cancers.

Your male APBT should be neutered. He will be a better dog for it, although any potential for aggressiveness will not be completely eliminated. One thing that will not exist for a neutered male dog is the tendency to travel in search of females in heat. As mentioned before, a loose APBT is often a dog that may not be long for this world. If you know that an escaped APBT is dangerous to himself and possibly to other dogs, and neutering can help curb the desire to roam, what more do you need to know?

One problem that many male owners of male dogs have is a heightened sense of "I can't do that to my dog" syndrome. First of all, you won't be doing anything to your dog except helping him out. The veterinarian will perform the relatively simple operation. If you have your APBT neutered early in life, the habits and patterns of unneutered male dog behavior will not become too deeply engrained. Neutering also virtually eliminates the chance of your pet developing testicular or prostate cancer.

Your APBT as an Adult

Your APBT will rapidly go through puppyhood into adolescence and then into adulthood. If your adult APBT has been thoroughly socialized, he is now capable of going most places with you without too much chance of ugly incidents. If you go to the same public places that your dog visited with you as a puppy, he already is familiar with many of the sights, sounds, and smells that will normally be a part of those places.

Just because your APBT is now an adult does not mean that you can forego ample time spent with the dog. The lessons begun when the APBT was small will now pay off in a well-behaved, full-grown dog. You will find that it was much easier to bend the little puppy to your will than an adult dog, but that does not mean that learning or training stops. In addition to reinforcing what your APBT already knows, adulthood is a time when many training options may be right for your dog.

Consistency was important for your pup and it is important for your adult dog. You should continue doing the same things that helped the youngster learn. The basic training lessons (see page 117) should be regularly reviewed. These lessons will be the foundation for much of the other training you do with your APBT. Nothing is more important to ensuring the people you meet that your dog is no threat than its calm demeanor and willingness to obey you. If you haven't instilled these lessons, and many others, in your puppy, you may never see them in your dog.

One interesting point about owning an APBT is the difference in strangers' response to the adult versus their responses to the puppy. People always love to be near your puppy. That may not always be the case when they realize that the well-behaved, medium-sized dog with you is an American Pit Bull Terrier.

Be prepared for this change in attitude and let the quality of your dog ultimately win people over.

Because there are many different colors in the APBT, some people may not immediately recognize your dog for what he is. Whether you have had the ears cropped or not seems to make little difference in the public-recognition factor with some people. How you handle this will be up to you. Some APBT people, though not ashamed of the breed of their dog, always tell strangers that the dog is an American Staffordshire Terrier or a Boxer-mix. This is ironic because some Amstaff people, perhaps seeking to bask in the glow of the APBT charisma, sometimes refer to their AKC-registered Amstaffs as APBTs or even as "pit bulls!"

Part of the Family

Your adult APBT will be much better off if it is a key part of your family. Some of the problem "pit bulls" are APBTs that have been isolated from their families and have become bored, lonely, or frustrated in a backyard kennel. As your dog matures, strive to find more ways to involve the dog in your life and that of your family.

• If permissible, and if the situation is good for the dog, take your APBT to work with you.

• Take your APBT on weekend outings and extended vacations (see Traveling with Your APBT, page 104).
• Where appropriate and advisable to do so, let your APBT be a part of your regular recreational activities.
• Introduce your friends and houseguests to your dog, although you may want to put your pet in its crate on some occasions.
• Continue to socialize your adult APBT, much as you did when he was a puppy.
• Perhaps you will want to look into some of the activities that you and your APBT can do together: obedience, agility, weight-pulling, and others (see page 125).
• Even if you have a large fenced backyard, continue to walk your APBT in public.
• Every few months teach your APBT a new command and add repetitions of that command to your dog's complete repertoire that you thoroughly review at least weekly.
• Spend quality time with your adult APBT at home every day and encourage your family members to do the same.

Exercise and Your APBT

Your APBT comes from a long line of canine athletes. Don't let your dog vegetate. For his physical and mental good, you should be certain that the dog gets good exercise, if not daily, then several times a week on a regular schedule.

Your APBT could benefit from long walks, jogging with you—on lead, of course—and from chasing flying disks and balls in the backyard. Children are good exercise companions for APBTs. Some game-bred breeders hang old tires from trees and let the dog exercise by jumping up and latching on with his teeth. APBTs really seem to enjoy this. One controversial piece of exercise equipment used by some APBT breeders is a treadmill. It is only controversial because some dogfighters have used treadmills as a part of their exercise regimen. Some law enforcement officers have confiscated such treadmills with the view that such equipment is dogfighting and dog-training paraphernalia. That doesn't explain all the non-APBT people who also use treadmills so their pets can get ample exercise.

APBTs actually don't have the "jaws of death" that have been widely publicized, but their jaws are strong and they do need tough chew toys. One dog expert suggests old bowling balls that you can get for free at most bowling alleys. After thoroughly washing the ball, put peanut butter, cheese, or some canned dog food in the finger holes. The dog will smell the treat and will push the ball around all day trying to get to it. This suggestion works best outside, especially if you have a flat (and fenced) backyard. You can easily wash whatever remains of the food treats out of the finger holes after your APBT has enjoyed

rolling the bowling ball around all afternoon.

Your APBT as an Older Dog

Just as your puppy grew into splendid adulthood, so will your adult APBT age into senior dog status. Barring serious illness or accidents, your APBT may live 15 years or more. Other than getting a little grayer around the muzzle and

slowing down a step or two, age doesn't have to be a debilitating time for your American Pit Bull Terrier. Because of the hardiness of this breed, with proper care and regular veterinary medical attention, most of the senior years should be good ones.

There are a number of ways that you can help your APBT live a fuller and longer life.

• From puppyhood through to your APBT's last year, regularly schedule veterinary exams.

• Follow your veterinarian's advice faithfully.

• Visit the veterinarian as early as possible after an illness or injury is discovered.

• Make regular exercise part of your dog's lifestyle and yours.

• Make the environment APBT-friendly and never let your dog roam free.

• Have your APBT spayed or neutered.

• Brush your APBTs teeth, starting in early puppyhood, several times a week, daily if possible (see teeth care, page 102).

• Keep your APBT out of any fights.

• Be consistent in how you deal with your dog; inconsistency can stress some dogs.

• Feed a good, premium dog food, don't switch foods quickly or often, never feed table scraps, and avoid giving too many treats.

• Don't feed your pet too much; let him drink a lot of water and then get involved in strenuous exercise (see gastric torsion or bloat, page 151).

• When traveling, always have your pet either in his crate or safely secured by a doggy seat belt. Never let your dog run around free in your vehicle and never let your dog ride in the back of an open pickup truck without appropriate safety restraints.

• Even if your APBT is large and sturdy, never let small children ride on the dog's back.

• As your APBT ages, gradually slow down, but do not eliminate, the exercise, and give the old dog extra attention.

• If you have several dogs, be sure that the younger and stronger dogs don't push the older dog around.

• Never leave your APBT in a situation where some dog-hating lunatic can do harm to it.

• Never leave your APBT in an automobile, even with the windows partially rolled down, when the temperature rises above 65°F (18°C).

• Be certain that all the members of your household recognize the signs of aging and adjust their activities accordingly.

Euthanasia

Then the day comes that never should come in the life of any APBT, the day when the decisions get much harder and the realities get much harsher. You spend a lot of time just communing with the best old dog you've ever known. Your heart skips a beat every time you see the old dog sleeping and you have to do a double take to be sure the dog's chest is still going up and down. Somehow you sense that the dog knows you can't make everything as it was before.

The care you give this loving, breathing, adoring creature may be directly proportional to the length and quality of this dog's time with you. When the time comes to make the hard decision, do it, but do it knowing you have done your best to make everything up until now the best it could be in terms of caring for your pet and companion.

Keeping Your APBT Looking Good

Pit dog people would have you believe that appearance was never a big breeding consideration in the old days. "The winning dog always looked good to its owner," a former pit dog expert stated. Ironically, the modern APBT has become a beautiful breed even if the pit didn't require good looks.

In either gender, a well-muscled APBT looks good to many dog fans. Even those who aren't interested in the APBT as a breed to own often do a double take at a particularly good-looking dog. Not much emphasis was put on looks in the early years and form followed function, but the form of the APBT is one of smooth, muscular, clean-cut lines. The short and rather hard coat allowed rippling muscles and strong structure to show through.

The APBT can be virtually any color. This is not true of most of the other bull-and-terrier breeds. Even the close-cousin breed, the American Staffordshire, disallows all-white or mostly white dogs and dogs that

are all red in color. Many of the colors and markings of the APBT are beautiful with great blending and great contrast possibilities. Good grooming will always accent any APBT's appearance.

Grooming

Grooming your APBT is not very difficult at all. Start early with your APBT puppy when you are much stronger than the puppy. Gradually the youngster will come to enjoy each phase of grooming and the process will be much easier when your dog is older and stronger.

Brushing: Take some time to brush and go over your APBT a few times a week. Use a medium to soft bristle brush and check for parasites, scratches, and other minute problems as you brush. This can also be part of the quality time that you and your dog should spend together on a daily basis.

Bathing: Regular brushing will eliminate much of the need for too-frequent bathing. When you do bathe your APBT, use a mild shampoo made specifically for dogs because shampooing can dry a dog's skin by depleting natural oils. Don't let shampoo get into the dog's eyes, ears, or mouth. Wash the face, nose, and ears very gently with a soft cloth. Be sure to thoroughly rinse the entire dog of all shampoo residue.

Nail care: Regular walks on streets and sidewalks can help wear nails down, but if these walks are on grass and earth, the nails will need more attention. If your dog's nails are too long, you can actually hear them clicking as the dog walks across a hard surface. Your veterinarian can handle nail trimming on regular visits, but you should learn to keep the nails trimmed down. Decide which type of nail clipper you prefer and practice on matches and wood stems until you can cut off the pieces you want to remove. Don't trim too much or the nail will bleed. Your veterinarian or someone at a good pet product store can demonstrate to you (on your own APBT) how to actually trim nails. Also, get a good emery board or nail file to smooth out the trimmed nail edges. Frequent filing for a few minutes after you have brushed your dog will eliminate most trimming.

Ear care: Your APBT's ears may be cropped (cut in a special APBT manner) or left uncropped. Many dog people feel that some breeds look much better cropped—the Doberman is a good example. The APBT actually looks good both ways. (Cropping began in pit days to remove some ear length so a dog's opponent could not get a good grip.) When you regularly brush your APBT, carefully go over his ears checking for the presence of parasites (ear mites and ticks), dirt, foreign objects or small injuries. Using a soft cloth or a baby wipe, clean the internal part of the ear, but don't delve too deeply or rub too hard.

Teeth care: Another plus of brushing sessions is the opportunity to look at your APBT's teeth. This dental inspection is another task that is best started early in a pup's life. Carefully observe the overall condition of the teeth, gums, and throat. Even if you feed dry dog food and your dog plays with dental care chew toys, both of which can help keep plaque away, you will need to use a soft toothbrush with toothpaste designed only for dogs. Be very gentle with your puppy and slowly help him adjust to tooth brushing. Many health problems start with poor dental care. It may seem odd to brush your dog's teeth, but he will be healthier and his breath will be better too.

Feet: During your brief brushing and toothbrushing sessions, also check the dog's feet. Look at the pads for cuts and abrasions, and look between the toes for such foreign objects as small sticks, pieces of gravel, or grass and weed seeds.

Genitals: Check the dog's genitals for any unusual swelling or discharge. If the area around the anus has some dried fecal material adhering to the skin and hair, gently remove it, perhaps using a baby wipe.

Eyes: In your brushing sessions, carefully look at your dog's eyes. Some mucus will form in every dog's eyes from time to time, though it is not reflective of any health concerns; gently remove it with a soft cloth. Check the eyes for such foreign objects as grass seeds or dirt. Use the soft cloth to remove any objects that are in the eye. Leave inflammations, obvious eye injuries, and deeply embedded objects for your veterinarian to handle as soon as possible.

Nose: One area that is sometimes neglected in grooming is a dog's nose. Check your APBT's nostrils and nose skin (leathers) for injuries, foreign objects, or nasal discharge. If you find any of these, check with your veterinarian about the appropriate course of action.

The entire grooming and minimedical checkup should take no more than five minutes, three or four times a week. If you do this, your APBT will remain much healthier. Remember to start early to let a puppy come to expect all these grooming activities.

Traveling with Your APBT

Traveling with a pet can be a very enjoyable experience. It can also be a nightmare, often with tragic consequences. You need to put in some care and preparation before and while traveling with your pet. There are a number of important points to consider *before* you embark on a trip with your APBT:

• Very young, very old, or unwell pets should be left at home or boarded, rather than taken on a longer trip.

• Whether you take your APBT along with you should be decided solely on what is best for the pet. Remember that travel is stressful to a pet.

• If you aren't willing to restrain your pet in a carrier or by a doggy seat belt, don't take the dog on the trip. Minor fender benders or just a sudden stop can turn an APBT into a living missile that can crash through a windshield, slam hard against the dashboard, or into the humans in the car.

Author's Note: Due to modern restrictions, traveling by air with your APBT is probably not a good idea. As with traveling to other countries, there are just too many potential problems to address. If at all possible, leave your pet home with good friends/family or in a quality boarding facility.

• Never leave your APBT (or any other kind of dog) in a car on even a moderately warm day when temperatures are 65°F (15.6°C) or higher.

• Schedule travel breaks, especially on longer trips, every hour to give the APBT an opportunity to defecate or urinate, and to drink some water. *Always* put a collar and leash on your APBT when you make these short stops.

• Never let your APBT ride with its head out of the car window. Eye injuries are common in such conditions, when road debris is hurled up or when insects fly into the dog's eye.

• When using interstate rest areas, use only designated relief trails. If you are traveling with a very young puppy, *never* use these pet walks. Very young puppies may pick up some serious illnesses from dogs that have used these pet relief spots previously. Find a remote spot at the rest area or go somewhere else entirely to let your young puppy relieve itself.

• Be certain of the communities you are going to and through. Some places have strict breed-specific bans addressing APBTs and other related breeds. If you visit some of these places with a dog in one of the banned breeds, you could face a stiff fine or even have your pet taken away from you. Sadly, ignorance of the law is no excuse.

• If you are staying in hotels on your trip, always obey the rules. If animals are prohibited at a particular place, go somewhere else! Never try to slip your APBT in for the night and hope no one finds out; the one place you pick to pull this might just be in one of the anti-APBT places. Save yourself some grief and maybe your APBT's life and find a place that does accept well-mannered pets.

• Always get a veterinarian checkup and the required health certificate before you go on your trip. If you should run into problems, you want everyone to know that your pet has had all its shots, what other prescriptions the dog needs, and so on. Traveling to other countries may require very specific medical records, or it is even possible that you might get into another country with just a cursory look at your pet's medical records, but not have what you need to come back into the United States. Always "know before you go!" Be sure all of your pet's paperwork is in order and recently signed by the right people.

• Be sure that you bring any medications with you that your pet requires, clearly labeled by the veterinarian as to what they are and what they do.

• Have the addresses, fax numbers, and office and home numbers of your veterinarian and your attorney with you at all times in case a traveling problem occurs.

• Have all of the appropriate identification papers for your pet: rabies certificate, dog license, registration papers, some recent (and very clear) color photographs. Have someone who can write the language of the country you are visiting type out all pertinent information about your pet in the appropriate language as

well as English. Keep several copies (notarized!) of this multilingual information in several places: with your luggage, your passport, your wallet, and on your person.

• Have at least two forms of identification for your pet: a collar that stays on the dog at all times with your name and address on it, and a tattoo or microchip that also identifies your APBT.

• If you are not absolutely sure that you can get your APBT's regular food at your destination, then carry enough with you. Diarrhea and other food-related problems won't make the trip any easier on your pet.

Chapter Eleven
Training Your APBT

Training is both incredibly complex and surprisingly simple. The complexity of dog training deals with approaches and styles and ways to convey or communicate what you want your pet to do. The simplicity of training is made abundantly obvious after you have established a clear channel of communication with your pet. Once your APBT puppy understands what you want, your adoring young dog really wants to give it to you.

If you have never trained a dog before, then get help from the start in the form of an obedience class and/or a professional trainer. Training an APBT is so important that if you don't have a big enough budget to buy an APBT *and* afford appropriate training, don't buy the puppy until you can also spring for the training.

The Importance of Training

Owning any dog and not giving that dog ample training is really sad. Owning an APBT and not giving him ample training borders on absolute insanity. Any untrained dog can be a definite liability. An untrained APBT can be the ultimate liability. Just imagine it: You have a powerful animal that you cannot control. Put this same animal into a social climate that already has irrational fears about just such uncontrollable, powerful animals and it is certain disaster.

Don't own an untrained APBT! An untrained dog will never reach his potential as a pet and companion. The APBT can be an excellent pet and companion, and it seems a real shame to let all his attributes go to waste by not training the dog.

Most APBTs are quite easy to train. They bond quickly and strongly to their family and really want to please these humans. The main issue is how to convey just what would please the humans to the young and impressionable APBT that wants to know just what to do.

Dogs without formal training from their significant human will substitute their own informal training. After said dogs have trained themselves, based on what they perceive life's lessons to be, the same dogs will proceed to train their humans. This is the nature of dog training, which in the wild is handled by the relatively complex concept of pack behavior. Pack behavior remains the crucial element in dog training. It is crucial because your puppy already is instinctively geared to understand it. Now all that is required is to gear *you* to understand it and apply it with your puppy.

Understanding Pack Behavior

Wolves and Chihuahuas, Great Danes and Yorkshire Terriers, wild dogs and your APBT are all predisposed to be trainable using the concepts of pack behavior. Pack training actually begins well before a puppy leaves the warm confines of the whelping box where the puppy and his littermates were born. The

best dog trainer that your APBT will ever encounter, his mother, is already in charge and training classes are ready to begin. The litter is your pup's first pack and his mother is the first leader-of-the-pack. Adaptation to pack behavior begins early and will continue throughout your APBT's life.

Even though your American Pit Bull Terrier will become an important part of your household, the important affiliation in the dog's young mind will be related to his position in the pack. In the wild, dogs or wolves will remain together in order to work together for survival. In a pack, each animal has his own particular place or level. The pack is a hierarchy where each member falls in line below the canine above him in the pack's pecking order. The pack leader fills the alpha position or number one spot. This position in packs of wild dogs and wolf packs is usually filled by the strongest and smartest male, but in the case of your pup's litter, a strong and smart female will occasionally take the top role. The alpha dog is dominant over all other members of the pack. The next strongest and smartest animal usually fills the beta position. The beta dog is dominant over all other members of the pack, except the alpha dog. So the pack structure goes from the strongest down through the ranks of the lesser animals to the very newest members of the pack, the puppies.

The pack is a perfectly natural social order and has worked well for countless generations of wild canines. The pack is just as natural for you and your APBT puppy and will work just as well for both of you. The most important thing to remember about this system is that in the world of humans and dogs, all humans must be higher in the pecking order than all dogs are.

Do not misinterpret the pack as some sort of power game where everybody gangs up on a poor defenseless puppy. Your pet's mental equilibrium is based in part on his social standing and balance within whatever pack he may belong. In his original home with mother and siblings, even for the few weeks the youngster lived there, a clear pack formation occurred. After leaving mother and littermates behind, your puppy will come to consider *you* to be the alpha dog of his life and all of the others in your household to be members in his pack.

Understanding that *all* humans must be above *all* dogs in a family pack is crucial in settling the order issue in the family-pack. You or some other strong and responsible human must be the aggressive pack leader. Unless there is a clear leader, it is conceivable that the pup, when older, might move to occupy the top spot. A dog cannot be permitted to believe he is above a human. It is easy to understand how some dogs might conceivably punish children that appear to the dog to rank lower in the pack than the dog. In the wild, a subservient pack member that gets out of line would be attacked and punished by any member above him on the ladder.

Chain of Command

The pack is a natural chain of command. You, as the alpha leader, will have to make certain that the chain is strong and that all links are connected. For example, if your young APBT is not allowed to get up on the couch in the family room, all humans in the household must enforce that rule. If you and your spouse make the APBT get off the couch, but one of your children, in your absence, doesn't enforce this family rule, the young dog may interpret that this permissive child is not dominant enough to enforce this rule. This one exception could start a gradual weakening of the chain of command. All humans must be consistent with the puppy if all humans are to remain in places above the puppy in the pack.

The Mother Dog's Training Model

Your pup's mother will be the best trainer that the puppy will ever have. If you and your family want to make the entire process of training much easier, you will use the mother dog as your guide. The mother taught her litter of little APBTs many things during their brief time with her. Some of the lessons she taught them will be followed throughout the life of each littermate. In her training methodology, the mother used the following training tools.

• She was *fair*; she maintained her own level of fairness. Each puppy was bound by the same rules and the same punishments.

• She meted out punishment *without anger.* Punishment was meant to correct and educate, not to injure her puppies.

• She acted *immediately.* A wrong-doer received instant punishment that was effective in connecting the act with the consequence of the act in the mind of a puppy with a short-attention span.

• She acted *appropriately.* The actions of the mother dog fit the misdeed of the puppy. She didn't inflict a serious bite for a minor infraction, nor did she bark constantly at a miscreant pup.

• She acted *consistently*. Her puppies were treated consistently with the same level of motherly displeasure expressed for a specific mis-behavior each time that misbehavior occurred. Puppies cannot learn right from wrong if what is right keeps changing.

• She acted out of *love.* Reprimands were carried out in an atmosphere of love and nurturing. The mother instinctively did what she had to do in order to prepare her offspring for their own entry into the world.

These training elements—fair-ness, lack of anger, immediacy, consistency, and love give any dog trainer a strong basis on which to build a trusting relationship. Canines learn by having the things they do right rewarded and the things they do wrong corrected. This is the simple part of the training process: Reward good behavior and correct bad behavior. The pack functions in exactly this same way. If pups do wrong, everyone above them in the pack can correct them.

The mother dog communicates just what her pups may do. She does this by the use of good and bad stimuli. Though approaches vary, this system of rewarding the positive and correcting the negative is the basis of most dog-training systems. Some training models are harsher than others when providing correction; other systems use treats as rewards for good behavior. There are all sorts of training types between the overly strict and the overly lenient forms. A good dog trainer can take almost any type of dog training and, by using this training type consistently and exclusively, make progress with it. What a trainer cannot do is to make any progress by being too strict sometimes and too lenient sometimes with the same dog. Consistency, one of the training examples from a pup's mother, has room for one type of training, but not more than one.

The rudiments of training can begin when a puppy is brought into his new home. These rudiments include initial house-training and crate-training with the possible inclusion of paper-training. These very necessary things should probably take precedence over teaching a puppy basic commands. In the opin-ion of most trainers, house-training and crate-training can start immediately. Basic command training (the *sit, stay, down, come,* and *heel*) can begin at about two months of age.

Crate-training

One of the first lessons that a mother dog teaches her older puppies is not to urinate and defecate in the den area in which they were born. This instinct comes from a mother's desire not to draw predators to the den because of the odors emanating from her puppies' bodily wastes. Denning behavior, especially for a mother canine about to whelp (give birth to puppies), is extremely strong. In the wild, a den becomes the animal's home, refuge, and nursery. Dens can be anything from a cave among some rocky outcroppings, a dugout area under the roots of a tree, the abandoned den of some other animal, or a shelter under branches or vines in a thicket. All of these dens have some common properties; they are secluded and hidden, often underground, defensible places where a dog or wolf can fight with its hindquarters protected from a rear attack, relatively close to water, used in hottest summers and coldest winters and all times in between, used both day and night, recuperation places for wounded, sick, or tired animals, places of rest and refuge.

Remember: Normal, healthy adult animals never defecate or urinate in their dens.

Dens are necessary for wolves and wild dogs; they are also necessary for domesticated canines, such as the American Pit Bull Terrier. Crates are man-made dens for pets in the home. The term *crate* can also be used to refer to cages, inside pens, inside doghouses, and airline-type carriers. To crate-train essentially means to accustom a young dog to any of the above enclosures. More specifically, crate-training means to use the crate as a place of rest and relaxation for the pet. Most important, the crate should be the place where a puppy should sleep.

Crate-training is a great aid to housetraining (see Housetraining, page 113) because of the mother dog's early lessons about not soiling the place the pups use as a den. An older puppy—as in the case of an older wolf cub—would be severely chastised for fouling the place where it is to sleep. Therefore, crate-training takes advantage of two great instinctual behaviors possessed by canines around the world: a strong desire to have a place that serves as a den, and the desire to keep that denning place clean.

If you as a dog trainer encourage these instinctive behaviors in your young APBT, you will find that not only will the dog learn the appropriate places for relief breaks, but he will also use the crate as a place to go to get away from the hubbub of the household. The crate will become a good temporary place to enclose your APBT. You may want to put the dog in his crate when guests are visiting, when you are doing household chores such as cleaning floors or painting, when a sick or injured pet needs a temporary hospital room, or when you just want to be away from your pet.

Crates are not little prisons that are cruel to your pet. As noted, if left to his own devices, your dog would invariably find a denning location. Crates are merely attractive ways to bring dens indoors and make use of the attending behaviors to make dogs better inside companions. There are some important things you should know about the effective use of crates:

• You and your family need to keep the right attitude about crates and their positive uses.

• Buying a crate is a little tricky. Decide whether you want a cage, crate, or carrier. Buy a crate to fit the adult dog your APBT pup will become. Build or purchase partitions to keep the crate the right size for the puppy as it grows—just enough room to turn around and stretch out comfortably. Too large a crate leaves room for a puppy to relieve himself in one corner and sleep in the other.

• Place your APBT's crate in a quiet, but not isolated place in your home, away from drafts, walkways, and direct sunlight.

• Observe your APBT, and if the youngster looks tired, place him in his crate and shut the door. This helps implant the idea that the crate is the place for sleep.

• Don't make getting out of the crate a big event. There should be no active praise or play with the newly released youngster for several minutes after he gets out of the crate.

• Don't use the crate as a place of punishment; never angrily grab a misbehaving youngster and banish him to his crate.

• Use crates when you travel with your pet (or a doggy seat belt and harness).

• Purchase some specially made mats for the floor of your APBT's crate. This will be a great comfort to the dog.

• Don't put food or water in the crate; toys and chew bones are fine. Other places are for eating and drinking; the crate is for rest and sleeping.

• Use the crate for the puppy's bedroom at night and don't let anyone give in to the whines of the youngster. The crate is where the dog sleeps.

• After training sessions with a puppy, put the young dog back into his crate for a few minutes before you begin a play session with him. This separates training, which should be serious, and play, which is not serious.

• Use the crate as an effective tool in housetraining your APBT puppy.

Housetraining

Crate-training and housetraining are two of the most important things your young APBT can learn. Ideally, the dog will learn both of these lessons quickly. These two lessons are

what makes the difference between an inside dog and an outside dog.

Housetraining can begin immediately when you bring your puppy home, but don't expect too much too soon. Some pups mature at a much slower rate and may need a little longer to learn the best relief spots.

The use of an outside relief spot is considerably preferable to papertraining. It is important to bond with your puppy as much as possible, even before you bring him home from the breeder. This bonding process will make the puppy love you and respect you as his alpha dog. Even a very young dog in a pack knows that his survival depends on pleasing those above him in the pack.

All living creatures have the need to release waste materials. Your APBT puppy is no different. When you can combine the great need to urinate and defecate with the great need to please you, housetraining will be very easy.

The Outside Relief Spot

Before you bring home your new American Pit Bull Terrier puppy, carefully study what outside areas are available to you. You want to pick a place in your yard that will be the primary relief spot for your APBT. This relief spot can be near a large rock, the base of tree, or a small bush. It needs to be a specific place that you and your family will always remember. Your puppy will find it another way, by scent.

If it is convenient for you to do so, obtain urine-soaked litter from the area in which your puppy lives at the breeder's. Put the used litter in a sealable plastic bag, and scatter the chosen relief site with some of the litter before you bring your puppy home. This will make this site identifiable to the puppy by its scent.

Canines are highly effective smellers. Their ability to pick up scents is thought to be hundreds of times greater than that of a human. The scent of a dog's feces and urine at a specific location tells him that this is the right place to relieve himself. You must make this immediate connection with your APBT puppy, which is why you put the used litter where you want the puppy to urinate and defecate.

When you have arrived home with your new puppy, go immediately to the relief site. Don't go inside your home. Don't show the puppy to your next door neighbor. Go immediately to the selected site. Don't talk much to the puppy on the way to the site. Put the youngster down where you have placed the used litter. Calmly and quietly wait until the puppy either urinates or defecates at that spot. This may take some time. When your puppy relieves himself, enthusiastically praise him. Make the pup feel that what he just did was the greatest thing that any puppy ever did. Be convincing.

Now you are free to take your new family member inside. Remember every time you take your puppy out to go through this same routine. Carefully observe the puppy. If he looks like he needs to go out, pick him up and go directly to the preset relief spot. This is not playtime or bonding time; this is potty time. Don't confuse the puppy by idle chatter. Quietly put the young dog down and wait for him to catch his own scent. When he does, he will probably mark that spot again with urine or with feces. When the puppy does that, heap on the praise.

The Puppy's Crate

Once the relief spot is firmly established in the puppy's mind—sometime during his first day at your home—introduce the crate. Calmly put the young APBT in it. Don't make a big deal about the youngster being in the crate; simply expect the puppy to stay in it at night.

The last thing that you do at night and the first thing you do in the morning is to take the puppy out to the relief site. When he does what he is supposed to do, praise him enthusiastically. Then go back inside and put the puppy back in the crate. If someone is at home during the day, the crate can be left open from time to time, but the puppy must be watched. If the pup starts to squat or looks nervous or loiters by the door leading outside, pick him up and go to the relief site. Even if you didn't make it in time, go there and wait until something happens.

Note: *Never strike a puppy or rub his nose in a potty mistake. This will make* the pup distrust you, which is something you don't ever want to foster.

Remember (see Crate-training, page 111) that the puppy will not want to mess where he sleeps. Whenever the pup is in his crate, he will be waiting for you, or some responsible adult, to come and let him out to go to the relief spot.

After Eating or Drinking

Whenever you feed your puppy or give him water, he should go out immediately. Small stomachs and bladders make quick trips outside necessary. Always follow the same procedure at the relief spot. The whole process will become habitual and the puppy will relieve himself there quickly, which is an advantage on rainy or cold nights.

Paper-Training

Paper-training is not nearly as effective for some dogs as crate-training and establishing an outside relief spot, but sometimes paper-training is necessary. The problem with paper-training is that with it there are now two right places to go and one of them is inside. Paper-training is the only alternative when no one is at home for several hours each day.

Follow these steps to make paper-training work well:
• Save the black-and-white sections of your newspaper.
• Choose a small room that can be almost solely devoted to the puppy, and cover the floor of that room with several layers of paper.

• Place the puppy's crate in one part of the small room and put some of the puppy's used litter in the opposite corner.
• Put food and water near the crate and far away from the relief corner.
• Pick up only the top layer or so when you remove the waste- and urine-stained paper. The all-important scent stays behind to tell the pup where to go.
• If you want to use an outside location too, you can do so. It is a bit harder to housetrain a puppy with two right places, but it can be done.
• As the puppy grows older, you can gradually eliminate the paper-training site and go exclusively outside, with paper-training as a convenient, but not great, alternative.

About Mistakes

When a young puppy can't get to the paper or to the outside spot soon enough, mistakes will occur. Many pet owners make the mistakes a million times worse by ignoring them.

If your puppy messes up, you must clean the mess immediately. Get some product from a pet supply store that will *neutralize* the scents in the urine or feces. Forget about home cleaning agents; they kill germs, but they don't get the scent out. If you don't get the scent out, the smelling ability of your puppy will convey to it that there are several right places to go because its nose tells it so. If you have carpet and are not sure if the puppy relieved himself

in several places, you must still get the smell neutralized: Buy (or rent) a black light from a pet products store. When the room is completely dark, bring out the black light and it will reflect urine spots. Mark those spots and clean them and then neutralize the scents. If you miss any spots, your puppy will find them for you and you'll still have to do the cleaning and neutralizing. Some dogs are harder to housetrain than others, but this method will surely work with any healthy puppy.

Pretraining Lessons

Because training really must fit both the trainer and the trainee,

there are some things you must remember to make your training effective.

• Your role is that of the alpha dog.

• Set a regular time for training each day.

• Each session shouldn't be much longer than 15 minutes.

• The focus of each session should be solely on training.

• Avoid busy and distracting times and places for doing the training.

• Training is serious, not just an extension of playtime.

• Set a clear (yet attainable) goal before each session and stay with it.

• Be consistent in training, including rewards.

• Correct immediately.

• Be patient with your young American Pit Bull Terrier.

Appropriate Training Equipment

Collar: Obtain the right size training or "choke" collar and then use it correctly and humanely. Such collars should be put on the pup just before the training session and taken off the puppy when the session is over. Use a sharp, but not overly hard, tug accented with the training buzzword "*No!*"

Leash: You should also have a 1-inch-wide (2.5 cm) training lead or leash that is 6 feet (1.8 m) long. It can be made of leather, nylon, or cotton webbing. This leash is exclusively for use with the training collar and not for walks in the park with your puppy or for any other reason.

Command voice: Practice your "command voice." Don't shout. Speak clearly and in a voice that is somewhat firmer than your regular voice. This voice is used to clearly communicate to your APBT that you are in a different aspect of the alpha role and that the pup should pay attention. As with the training collar, this voice is used to get the pup's attention; it is not your opportunity to intimidate a defenseless puppy.

Treats: Keep treats in a sealed sandwich bag in your pocket. Many handlers believe that praise is enough; other handlers believe that a small food treat works even better. Smart trainers probably use a little of both. The sealed bag is to keep the treat scent from distracting the puppy during the session.

Always remember the mother dog's training style:

1. Correct immediately.

2. Be consistent.

3. Never lose your temper.

4. Reward enthusiastically.

5. Be patient and remember that this is a puppy that really wants to please you.

Five Starter Commands

There are five basic commands you will want your APBT to learn. Since control of your APBT is one of the most important things you want to accomplish, these five commands will serve that purpose well. They are *sit, stay, heel, down,* and *come.* Each of these commands is a little different in focus and will require your puppy to mentally stretch in different directions. It is also important that the commands are easy to teach and easy to learn. They are commands that you can use in regular life with your APBT and could keep the dog from getting into trouble or getting injured or killed.

The Sit

Of course, your puppy already knows how to sit, but the key to this command is to get the dog to do what he knows how to do at the time you want it done. The *sit* is an excellent simple command with which to start and a good place to go back to so that each lesson ends on a properly executed command and the subsequent reward (praise or treat): Lift the pup's head upward slightly while putting gentle downward pressure on his hindquarters, saying "Sit" at exactly the same time his head goes upward and rear end goes downward. Done in this manner, the puppy learns both the motion you want and the command for it in a few short sessions.

Put the collar with attached leash on your pet's neck.

1. The puppy is positioned on your left, next to your left leg.

2. Take up (into your right hand) all but about 12 inches (30 cm) of the extra leash length.

3. With the leash still in your right hand, make a firm but smooth continuous, gentle upward move.

4. With the leash, in the same continuous move, lift your pup's head.

5. As you make the upward move with your right hand, gently press down with the hand on the pup's hindquarters.

6. While the upward pull lifts the pup's head and the downward push causes his hindquarters to go to the ground, using the dog's name, say, "*Rocky, sit*."

7. Reward the puppy while he is still sitting.

Using this same outline, practice the *sit* several times, but don't overdo it or leave the pup sitting for too long. The *sit* is a crucial command. Most other commands start with the dog in this position, put

there by you. Always start and end your training sessions with a few *sits*.

The Stay

After your American Pit Bull Terrier fully understands the *sit*, the next command, a very important one, is the *stay*. The *stay* is crucial for an APBT. You want this command to be obeyed with just the same amount of "no-quit" that the American Pit Bull has inbred into him. If all your other control measures fail at some point, the simple stay command may be the only thing that will keep your pet alive or out of a serious altercation. The *stay* has a negative built into it for a young dog; the pup adores you and wants to be with you, right by your side, but now you tell the youngster that he must be some distance away from you and that he must remain there.

1. The *stay* begins with the puppy in the comfortable sit position, next to your left leg.

2. Keep gentle pressure on the leash to keep the pup's head slightly up.

3. With the pup in the *sit*, say in a firm, alpha voice, "*Rocky, Stay!*"

4. As you give the command, step straight forward, leading with your right foot.

5. At the same time, bring the palm of your left hand down in front of your pup's face.

The *stay* will require some practice, but your APBT should catch on.

Practice for short periods, doing everything the same each time. If the puppy moves out with you, stop and go back to the sitting position and start the *stay* over again. If the pup doesn't get it right away, don't get frustrated. Always end each training session with some *sits* and praise. If the pup stays at all, praise him where he stayed.

As the *stays* get longer and the puppy is doing well, you can insert the release word "*Okay*" to let the pup know he can join you and be rewarded.

The Heel

Your APBT should learn to walk next to your left leg without lagging behind or surging ahead. The pup learns a useful way to stay close to you and you don't have to contend with a strong pup pulling ahead. Because of the strength of your APBT, the *heel* is another very important command. It is also important to keep a strong dog from towing along smaller children and lighter adults on walks.

1. The pup is in the *sit* position, next to your left foot.

2. Hold the lead, still attached to the training collar, in your left hand.

3. Step off with your left foot.

4. As you step forward, say "*Rocky, heel.*"

5. If the pup doesn't move out as you do, snap the coils of extra leash against your left leg and keep walking.

6. If the puppy stays with you, praise him as long as he stays by your left leg.

7. If the pup stops or veers away, stop and start the lesson over.

The key elements are: (1) the pup is sitting in place, (2) you are holding the lead in your left hand, (3) you step off, this time leading with your left foot, (4) you snap the leash against your leg to get the puppy moving, (5) you praise as you move, and start over if the puppy stops or veers.

different kind of command that can be misused and untaught.

You could use a longer leash and say "*Rocky, come*" as you gradually and gently bring the puppy toward you. Perhaps a better way is to kneel and open your arms wide and say enthusiastically, "*Rocky, come!*"

There are several other important points about this command:

• You can overwork it by calling the dog to you too often.

• *Never* associate this command with something negative such as punishment. If you call your dog to you for punishment, you can teach him to "un-come" pretty quickly; therefore, always go to the dog if you have to correct him.

• Use the command "*Rocky, come!*" occasionally when something else is on the pup's mind, as when he is playing.

• Always reward the pup when he comes to you.

The Down

The *down* is another potential life-saving command. It starts in the *sit* and requires the puppy to go downward from the *sit* onto his belly and then to *stay* there.

1. With your right hand pull the leash (and pup's head) gently downward.

2. Move your left hand in front of your pup's face in a strong, repeated downward motion, as if bouncing a ball.

3. As you do the other actions, firmly give the command, "*Rocky, down.*"

Later, after the dog has mastered the *down*, give the release word, "*Okay.*"

The Come

This command is more difficult than it appears. It might seem that all dogs know how to come to their owner, but the trick is getting them to come when called. The *come* is a

Using a Professional Trainer

As important as it may be for you to understand the rudiments of basic commands, it is even more important that you and your APBT engage the services of a professional dog trainer. A professional

trainer will help you train your dog faster and more easily than you could probably do alone.

Some American Pit Bull Terriers can be somewhat headstrong. If you don't impact immediately with such a pup, you may be in for a long, hard training road. It is therefore important to find a professional trainer who has had experience with APBTs through basic training to obedience, if possible. Budget the money for this professional even before you purchase your APBT pup. You will not regret the amount spent. The skill and experience of a professional trainer will be a bargain when you and your APBT are working well together.

A professional trainer will be a great aid in helping to choose a path for your puppy regarding the many activities available to the versatile APBT. A trainer will have a broad understanding of, and often specific experience in, many of the fields of interest outside of obedience training, such as agility or weight pulling.

Your professional trainer will give you greater confidence in owning an APBT. You will have a mentor in whom to confide. He or she will help ease any other areas of faint misgiving that you may have about owning an APBT, and, through the learned eyes of a good trainer, you will be able to see the true potential of your APBT.

Chapter Twelve

Activities for You and Your APBT

Your American Pit Bull Terrier and his versatility will open new doors to you. Many of these doors may include activities in which you have never participated, but not every APBT will be equally good in all areas. There are two ways that you can align yourself with an APBT and some of the many activities available:

1. You can purchase the best APBT puppy available, see what aptitudes this youngster has, and then try the activities that seem to best suit your dog.

2. Before you get your APBT, while you are studying about several breeds and the APBT in particular, you could visit conformation dog shows, weight pulls, obedience events, and the like. If one or more of these activities interest you, look to breeders in these groups for the pup you want.

Conformation Dog Shows

Both the United Kennel Club (UKC) and the American Dog Breeders Association (ADBA) have sanctioned conformation dog shows in which APBTs may compete. Visit a number of shows to get the feel and the atmosphere of these competitions.

Dogs are entered in classes according to age, gender, dog show experience, and so forth. Each APBT, in his best physical form, is judged against the written standards (see the UKC Standard, page 53).

Both of these organizations have standards, which are written descriptions of the perfect dog that are geared toward the working dog requirements for the APBT.

If you believe that conformation dog shows are for you, seek out some breeders of APBTs that have excelled in such shows. It is unusual to get a top-quality show dog out of a litter than has been bred for some other activities, such as hunting or agility. Since there are some American Staffordshires being shown at UKC shows, take a look at this breed for yourself. It is possible that you could find a pup that is eligible for double registry. This puppy would be from parents that are registered as APBTs in the United

Kennel Club and Amstaffs in the American Kennel Club. There are also some double-registered dogs in the UKC and in the American Dog Breeders Association.

Local clubs put on most dog shows and these can be all-breed shows or shows for only certain breeds, such as the APBT. Visit a number of dog shows; find a mentor among the show APBT breeders to explain the events to you. Shows are great fun, both watching and participating in.

Obedience Training

Obedience training is a wonderful option for your APBT for several reasons.

• Obedience is a great way to make use of your pet's many abilities.

• Your APBT wants to please you and obedience training is an in-depth way to build on your pet's love for you.

• Obedience training offers a number obedience titles than can be won by a hard working dog and owner. UKC titles are:

U-CD – United Companion Dog

U-CDX – United Companion Dog Excellent

U-UD – The United Utility Dog

Each of these levels has a group of training lessons and skills that must be mastered before moving on to the next level. Even if an APBT can complete only part of the basic level,

the dog is much better trained than a vast majority of the dogs not in obedience in the United States.

• Obedience work can be very hard, but the rewards are as good as anything in the dog-owning world. The United Kennel Club (see Useful Addresses and Literature, page 170) has all the information about this intense training and would be happy to share it with you.

Note: While nothing has been finalized at the time this is being written, some insurance companies are discussing a plan, not unlike non-drinkers' auto insurance, that would cut rates on homeowners with APBTs that have UKC obedience titles.

Agility Tests

Agility involves intense training and superb physical coordination with a dog timed against an intricate obstacle course. Jumps, tunnels, ramps, a seesaw, and a line of poles to weave in and out of are all part of the agility course. Agility is intended for good canine athletes and requires training to negotiate the course, but everything depends on the fire and drive of the individual dogs.

In addition to the obedience and exercise aspects, agility events are extremely colorful and a lot of fun for the humans and the dogs involved. The United Kennel Club has some agility events, as does the United States Dog Agility Association (see

Useful Addresses and Literature, page 170). More and more agility events are finding a strong audience of fascinated viewers.

Working an American Pit Bull Terrier off lead can lead to possible altercations with other dogs that are usually under the control of their owners when not actually competing. The level of training involved in agility events may be enough to control your dog. If you are not absolutely certain of your APBT's temperament, perhaps agility work should be avoided.

Weight Pulling

The American Dog Breeders Association has a weight pull contest exclusively for APBTs. Securely fastened within a padded harness, APBTs—and other breeds in weight pull events—are hitched to carts carefully weighted with specific poundage. All dogs involved in this activity have been conditioned and trained by gradually introducing more weight to the carts. No dog, no matter how strong that dog may be, should be allowed to attempt weight pulling without sufficient training and conditioning. Before attempting any pulls, weight pull contestants should be carefully warmed up.

This weight pulling can be done at home for enjoyment or for exercise for an active APBT dog. If a dog is good enough, there are competitive weight pulls. The American Dog Breeders Association (ADBA) has weight-pulling contests that are open only to APBTs. In these ADBA events, a weighted cart must be pulled by an APBT for a distance of 16 feet (4.9 m) with a one-minute time limit. If a dog wins, he receives credit, in the way of points, that will go to earn the "Ace" Weight Pulling Title. For top weight pullers, there is the "Ace of Aces" title.

While some uninitiated dog person might look askance at the rather small APBTs pulling heavy weights, the simple truth is that if the dog didn't want to pull the weight, he would simply stop. At a weight-pulling demonstration at an AKC show, I once saw an APBT pull a Nissan pickup truck loaded to the top of the truck's bed with bags of dog food, on a perfectly flat surface, the required 16 feet (4.9 m). The dog weighed about 65 pounds (29 kg) and was allowed to pull on a special rubberized mat for traction. When the American Pit Bull Terrier had completed the pull, his owner wanted to rush over to the dog to pet and reward him. On this occasion, the owner was delayed getting to the dog by a barricade that had been erected to keep the public off the pull track. Before the owner could get to the APBT, the happy dog jumped toward him and pulled the loaded truck another foot! Information about weight-pull organizations is included in Useful Addresses and Literature, page 171.

Hunting and Working Livestock

If hunting offends you, please go to another part of this book, as this one is about the perfectly valid activity for APBTs, hunting. As President Theodore Roosevelt pointed out to his daughter Ethel some people don't enjoy this activity. Roosevelt wrote of the hunting for mountain lions and lynx that was facilitated by the half-bred bulldogs.

Some hunters use APBTs to hunt wild boars. This has become a real activity of choice for owners of game-bred APBTs. The wild swine are widely spread throughout the United States and do damage to some crops and other farming activities. Hunting them has become a popular way for APBT people to test the gameness of the dog in a legal manner.

Famous scientist Dr. I. Lehr Brisbin has been active in the conservation effort to preserve certain animals that have long been a part of American wildlife. Dr. Brisbin, who is known for his studies of the Dingo, Australia's indigenous dog, discovered and has now preserved the Carolina Dog, the feral dog living in the United States. Dr. Brisbin has also been highly instrumental in studying the habits and the habitat of the wild pig. He told the author that although he has used APBTs and other dogs to catch and band wild swine, he has had great success with the Jack Russell Terrier in the same work.

The important element of hunting with an APBT is temperament. It would be impossible to hunt with dogs that were so busy fighting among themselves that they wouldn't or couldn't hunt.

Working livestock with the APBT is still done in areas where wild hogs and semiwild cattle range through tough terrain. Not unlike the bullbaiting of the ancient days, dogs latch onto noses of animals and pull them to the ground. Farmers then run up and get the dog away from the livestock, brand the livestock, medicate them, or round them up for slaughter.

Working livestock may not be something that you could get involved in after work or on the weekends, but APBTs are adept at this activity. As discussed, hunting is not for everyone—but then neither is the APBT.

Therapy Dog Opportunities

The Delta Society and other organizations have discovered the curative and comforting values of dogs and other pets with hospital patients, people in long-term care facilities, and with others on the hurting edge of life. For some deep-seated and inexplicable reason, dogs can bring comfort to those who are very sick. They can bring a touch of the familiar and familiarity to seniors in nursing homes.

After careful screening, involving a number of tests of temperament, insecurity, liking for people, and the ability to get along with different kinds of animals, some dogs are chosen as therapy dogs. Some of the therapy dogs are APBTs.

Volunteering your time and the time of your pet in an animal therapy program can be extremely rewarding. APBTs chosen for the programs have sound temperaments, are easily groomed, and have a genuine empathy for people in painful circumstances. Consider this unique giving experience when you evaluate activities to pursue with your American Pit Pull Terrier.

Chapter Thirteen
Feeding Your APBT

The Importance of a Good Diet

All dogs require food of sufficient quality to meet their nutritional needs. They also need food that will taste good and that they will readily eat. Dog foods must also be fed consistently; change may be good in some things, but not in dog foods and dog food feeding.

Without a good diet, American Pit Bull Terriers will not grow strong and vigorous. Humans have many dietary options; pet dogs can only eat what is provided for them. Without proper food, puppies will not grow into healthy adults. Some dogs that have been neglected nutritionally may also suffer in their mental development as well. Your APBT must depend on you for all his dietary requirements; you must understand what these requirements are and how to fill them.

Special Considerations

As an active breed, the APBT requires a diet that will meet the needs of an active lifestyle. The APBT is not usually an overly large breed, but it is still a dog of impres-sive physical proportions. While not hampered by the extreme rapid growth of some breeds, the medium-sized APBT must still be considered a breed that requires special dietary attention.

All aspects of a dog's health, appearance, vitality, and mental acuity are directly connected with the food he ingests. While an extremely hardy dog, the APBT still has certain conditions that require attention. As a short-coated breed, the emphasis in the APBT is not on a long, full coat as it is with Collies, Afghans, and others; yet the coat is always something of a signal of the overall condition of a dog. Blue, blue-and-white, and blue brindle are all common colors for the APBT. Blue is a dilute color, as is the light tan, some-times called cream. Some breeders believe the red-nosed red APBTs (a very popular color phase) are always representative of dilute col-oring. On average, blues and other dilutes have weaker coats and skin problems seem more prevalent in the dilutes. Inasmuch as good-qual-ity food, fed consistently, can help produce better skin and coat, then paying close attention to feeding is

important for APBT owners, especially the owners of dogs with dilute coloring.

Feeding an APBT requires attention during the different growth stages of his life. Puppies, struggling to build the body and muscles of the adult will need more good nutrition, as will active adults. At some point, growth is achieved and maintenance takes over. Also at some point, a dog's metabolism will no longer need the same foods for growth and maintenance. Obesity in older APBTs can be handled with food that is nutritionally sound, but lower in calories.

Balance—The Key to Good Nutrition

Because our dogs are totally dependent on us for all the food they eat, we must be absolutely certain that the diets we use for them

are balanced. Balanced dog foods are those that scientifically contain all the necessary protein, carbohydrates, fats, vitamins, and minerals the dog will need first to grow up, then to maintain an active and healthy metabolism.

The food must contain the right blend of the right things. Far too many dog owners are content to feed whatever is handy, available, expedient, and inexpensive. You should not do this. You must find that quality food that meets the requirements of your APBT. Along with balance, the food must be palatable; your dog must want to eat it!

There are a few major rules to follow in determining a successful feeding plan for your APBT. To avoid a poor diet, establish a nutritionally sound feeding regimen; adhere to these basic principles:

1. Feed your APBT a premium-quality, nutritionally balanced dog food and understand why it is so designated.

2. As long as a particular food is meeting your dog's need, be consistent and stick with it. Don't constantly jump around from brand to brand.

3. Don't overfeed, and *avoid table scraps!* There is no way that you can keep your APBT's diet balanced if the household leftovers end up in the dog's food bowl or in the dog's stomach. Your dog's food is balanced for dogs not for humans; the same thing works in reverse—human food will not meet the dog's nutritional needs.

Components of Canine Nutrition

There are several components that make up a sound, balanced nutritional feeding program for your APBT:

- Proteins
- Carbohydrates
- Fats
- Vitamins
- Minerals
- Water
- Owner Knowledge
- Owner Consistency

Proteins

Protein provides your APBT with the key amino acids that are so necessary for your dog's progression through the formative stages of his life, continued sustaining of healthy bone and muscle, the body's repair functions on bone and muscle, the production of infection-fighting antibodies, the production of needed hormones and enzymes that aid in natural chemical processes within the dog's body.

There are a variety of good sources for protein in a dog food. Chicken, poultry by-product meal, turkey by-product meal, meat meal, eggs, and fish are all sources of protein used in many quality dog foods. Poor-quality sources of protein are meat and bone meal and feather meal. In the guaranteed analysis percentages required on pet foods, listed on the bag, can, or package, protein is listed first. Discuss foods and feeding with experienced APBT people and with your veterinarian. Through this input and through your own study and observations, you should develop some valid ideas about appropriate levels and the best sources of protein in your dog's diet.

Carbohydrates

Carbohydrates provide usable fuel for your APBT's physical motor. Thoroughly cooked grain and vegetable products, and processed starches provide the source for most of the carbohydrates in premium-quality pet foods. Some specific high-quality carbohydrate sources are corn and rice. The next level of carbohydrates include: soy and soybean meal, corn gluten meal, and wheat. Wheat middlings are a poor quality source of carbohydrates. Along with fats, carbohydrates are the elements in your APBT's diet that give it usable energy.

Fats

The fats in your pet's diet provide a more concentrated energy source than do carbohydrates. In fact, the same amount of fat will provide *twice* as much usable energy as a like amount of carbohydrates. The fats in your APBT's meals deliver E and K essential vitamins and A and D. These are known as *fat soluble vitamins* and are useful in helping develop and maintain healthy skin and coat.

Fats have a low melting point, which aids in digestibility of the dog food. Meat sources such as chicken and other poultry, lamb, beef, and pork are all better sources of fats than are vegetable fat sources such as corn oil, soy oil, and wheat germ oil.

Fats are also of special importance in maintaining a dog's nervous system, but are equally significant in making dog foods more palatable. The dog foods that taste good are those more readily eaten by dogs, thus allowing a food to not only be nutritious and balanced but enjoyable. Finally, fat levels are often measured against the general activity level of a dog with the stresses of obedience work, breeding, and the show ring requiring more fats than those required for a less active dog.

Vitamins

While vitamins are certainly needed by your APBT for the general functioning of his body, vitamins are one of those good things that can be easily overdone. All the vitamins a dog normally needs are supplied in a regular diet of a premium-quality dog food. Unless your veterinar-

ian indicates otherwise, don't just impulsively add to the vitamin levels of a good food. Not only do additional vitamins generally not do any good, but also they can actually do harm.

Minerals

Minerals are important to the dog's normal functioning. Calcium and phosphorus are needed for the development and sustaining of healthy bones, teeth, and muscles; sodium and potassium help maintain normal canine body fluids and are used in the maintenance of a healthy nervous system. Like vitamins, minerals are not needed in huge amounts in your dog's regular diet. Consistent feeding of a good-quality dog food usually provides an adequate amount of minerals.

Water

An abundance of clean, fresh water is crucial to the health of your APBT; it should not be poor-quality, bacteria water or filled with algae. Make water as much a part of your pet's diet as any of the other elements mentioned. Keep water bowls full, clean, and always available for the good health of your APBT.

Owner Knowledge

Feeding any dog is an important undertaking. Not only do active, growing young APBTs need different rations than do average dogs, but your APBT's well-being throughout its life may largely depend on your knowledge of the food you feed him.

Your APBT must count on you for everything he eats. What you know of your dog's nutritional needs and which foods can best meet those needs will be a vital part—perhaps the *most* vital part—of caring for your pet.

Owner Consistency

Sadly, many dogs get to eat only whatever is available at the nearest convenience store. This might mean one food one day and another the next. While most dogs can *survive* on this incessant switching around of what they eat, they will not reach their genetic potential when there is no consistency in their diets.

When you have found a food that most meets the needs of your dog, stick with it. If your dog knows what food he can expect, he will be less likely to be a picky eater, and his system will be able to adjust to the formula of this particular diet. It is a human idea, not a canine one, that dogs love variety. Your pet will do better on the same, high-quality food, fed at regular times throughout much of his life.

Commercial Dog Foods

There are hundreds of pet food products available. Some are high-quality, balanced foods that may be just what you and your APBT are seeking. Others are inferior products that are best avoided by a dog owner in search of a nutritionally complete diet for a special pet.

Part of the knowledge component in your APBT's feeding plan is your learning how to read a dog food label and how to use this information to your pet's best interest. Along with the guaranteed analysis, which lists percentages of protein, fats, fiber, and moisture, the label contains a list, in descending order, of the ingredients that are in the dog food. The first ingredient listed will be the one most prevalent in the food, the next listed ingredient will be the next highest in amount, and so on down through the vitamins, minerals, and other items that go to make up the food.

Also on the label should be the manufacturer's recommended feeding amounts based on the weight of the dog. These are generally based on averages and do not take into account the special feeding needs of powerful and active dogs. Talk with your veterinarian and with your friends among experienced APBT breeders about how much food is generally right for your dog.

One of the pluses of using a premium-quality food is that these foods normally have a toll-free-number that can connect you with people experienced in canine nutrition. Don't hesitate to use these numbers to ascertain what food to feed or to ask questions about a food your APBT is already being fed.

Commercial dog foods generally come in three main forms: canned, semimoist, and dry. Each type has

some distinct advantages and disadvantages.

Canned Foods

Canned dog food, sometimes called wet food, is the most palatable and the most expensive way to feed your APBT. Canned food generally smells really good to a dog and usually is eaten with gusto, but because of its high moisture rating of between 75 to 85 percent, it can also spoil quickly at room temperature. For an APBT dog, a diet of exclusively canned food could be quite an expensive proposition. Additionally, the stool looseness and strong odor produced by feeding canned foods are usually the worst of any of the three forms of dog food.

Canned food is convenient and its long shelf life makes it easy to keep for extended periods of time. Canned food diets also tend to contribute to more dental problems than dry dog food. Most canned food is used as an additive or mixer with dry dog food for active breeds of dogs.

Semimoist Foods

Many of the semimoist dog foods come in shapes that appeal to human buyers rather than to dogs. Burgers, chops, and other meaty-looking configurations are used to sell the product, not to make it more nutritious or acceptable to a pet. Semimoist dog food is generally quite palatable and has a reasonably good storage life. They are generally the least natural of all foods, being laden with artificial colorings, scents, and so on. It is an expensive type of food for dogs to eat exclusively, but has uses in mixing with dry foods.

The stool quality with semimoist foods is a little better than with canned foods, but not up to the level of dry foods. Semimoist foods usually have a moisture rating of about 30 percent and are not used as a main diet by many APBT breeders. One advantage for semimoist can be in using the product as a treat or when a dog's normal appetite is a bit off. These neither wet nor dry foods also may have some use when traveling or as treats on a limited basis.

Dry Foods

The dog food form that may seem to be least what a dog would want or like is probably the best overall diet—dry dog food. It is the most cost-effective and most popular form of dog food, especially among large dog breeders. There are a good many dry foods on the market that can be truly described as complete dog diets with real nutritional balance.

Also, dry foods keep well without refrigeration, which isn't true for partially used canned and semimoist foods. Dry foods sometimes have a drawback in palatability but this problem has been studied and largely rectified by manufacturers of some of the premium brands that contain a poultry or lamb digest spray over the food to add taste.

Even with the modern palatability innovations, some dogs, especially those that have been fed only canned, semimoist, or table scrap diets, may have to be patiently taught to eat dry foods.

Because chewing dry dog foods makes more use of a pet's teeth, this form contributes somewhat to better dental health and tartar reduction on a dog's teeth.

Note: Information from some dry dog food makers notwithstanding, feeding dry food alone is not enough to keep your dog's teeth in good shape (see page 102).

When feeding premium-quality dry food, overall stool quality, in terms of firmness, stool size, and decreased odor, is usually the best. Digestibility is usually quite good. Puppies started on dry food readily eat it all their lives. Dry dog food, with only about 10 percent moisture, highlights the need for good, fresh water at all times.

Homemade Diets

Some dog experts with loads of dog nutrition and dog-feeding experience may experiment and attempt to develop their own dog foods, but with the high quality of modern premium foods, self-styled pet nutritionists have greatly declined in numbers. You simply cannot make a food as good as the top-quality premiums at a cost you will want to pay. Unless you are a trained canine nutritionist, or you are a dog breeder with a lot of experience and dog food knowledge, leave homemade diets alone. In the best of hands they may work as well as many commercial foods do. In novice or ill-informed hands, homemade diets are little more than nutritionally lacking meals of poorly disguised table scraps. Do your pet a favor—until you can do as good a job in canine diet formulation as the companies that have spent millions of dollars and decades of research developing their products, let dog food making stay with the experts!

Treats

Table scraps do not fit in a balanced canine diet. Table scraps will prevent a dog from eating the appropriate amount of his balanced food. In some cases and with some dogs, table scraps will throw the regular diet completely out of balance. It is also true that feeding table scraps to your APBT may very well cause your dog to expect to eat not only *what* you do, but also *when* you do, and possibly *where* you do. Your dog should eat from his dish at the regular time that you set for him to eat, and not from the table while you and your family are having a meal.

Dog biscuits: Among treats that *can* be given safely and appropriately to your APBT are quality dog biscuits. They are not only nutritionally good for the diet, but they are balanced to fit with the dog's regular diet. Follow the same rules with bis-

cuits that you do with dog food: Find a brand the dog will like, stay with it, and don't overdo. Less is better than more.

Chews: Non-food items such as those of nylon or rubber, do not necessarily fall into the category of treats. They will, however, be good for your dog. Along with providing some benefit in tartar removal—not to replace regular dental care— these items also help a teething puppy or a bored adult find a suitable alternative to the furniture to chew on.

Feeding APBT Puppies (Under Two Years Old)

Other than the regular dietary concerns about young APBTs, feeding APBT puppies isn't that different from feeding puppies of other breeds. It is important to remember that when you bring your APBT pup home you must be sure to get some of the *same* food he was fed at the breeder's. Of course, this recommendation is only applicable if the breeder has been feeding a quality food that is reflected in the quality of the puppies. Unless there are some serious food-related problems, as verified by your veterinarian, *never* change a puppy's food, unless you absolutely have no choice. If you continue the puppy on the same food that he has been eating, you will reduce the transition stress that

will already be in effect when your puppy leaves the only home he has ever known and moves with you to yours.

Young puppies under two years of age will need to be fed about four times a day with a quality food. As puppies grow older, the number of feedings can be reduced to three, and then finally to two as they approach adulthood.

Feeding Adult APBTs (Two to Five Years Old)

For some dogs adulthood comes more quickly than others. There are those who believe that an APBT will be near maturity at a little over one year. Some strains or families in this breed will mature at different rates of speed. Gradually decrease the frequency of your dog's feedings as he grows older. Normally, an adult dog will receive two feedings a day.

The amount and the number of daily feedings will also depend in part on the special conditions in the lives of you and your APBT. If yours is a prime show dog being actively campaigned at different locations each weekend, his needs will be different from the spayed or neutered APBT that lives a less active life. If your APBT is active in agility or weight pulling, your dog may need even more nutrition than a show dog does. The metabolism of some dogs, even from the same litter, may indicate that they will need more food than others will. Experience

with your particular dog is the only way you can come to understand all his specific needs.

Feeding Older APBTs (Seven Years Old and Older)

As your APBT ages, his metabolism will slow down. Along with growth and the amount of food needed, the aging rate also may differ from dog to dog. Sooner or later, at some point in his life, the dog will need less fat in his food. Many "senior" dog foods are designed for older canines. Spayed and neutered APBTs may require a diet much like that of older dogs regardless of the pet's age. The important point to remember in feeding older pets, spays, and neuters is that a fat APBT is not a healthy APBT. Not only does added weight require that the dog's internal organs work harder, obesity will also put more stress on a dog's feet and legs and joints. If you have any doubts about when your older dog needs a senior diet, consult with your veterinarian and with other APBT owners about their recommendations on this age-related problem.

When You Must Change Dog Foods

While various experts disagree on the length of time you should take to make a dog food change, one good way is to effect this dietetic transition over a month's time. This method stresses a gradual change. The first week of the month feed 75 percent of the current food with 25 percent of the new brand. Observe the dog's acceptance of the new ration. If the new food doesn't seem to cause any problems, feed 50 percent of each kind for the second and third week. The fourth week of the month, you should mix 25 percent of the old with 75 percent of the new. By the end of this time you should be able to start the next month on the entirely new diet. If you change your APBT's food slowly, you'll achieve better feeding results and fewer health problems.

Chapter Fourteen

The APBT and Health Care

The APBT will need specialized preventive and treatment measures not usually necessary for other dog breeds. As with so many aspects of this breed, a good preventive focus to anticipate health problems before they occur, a medical care "team" to deal with ongoing health issues or conditions that are unavoidable, and a specific medical plan are all needed to help insure your APBT's well-being.

Keeping Your APBT Healthy

Your APBT will need a team of concerned, APBT-knowledgeable people to make and keep his existence a safe one. This team will consist of you, the other members of your family, perhaps a trusted and experienced breeder, and of greatest value—your APBT's veterinarian.

You should learn about accident- and incident-prevention techniques and concepts. You will need to learn about parasites, disease,

and other medical conditions that may afflict your pet. An experienced APBT breeder may be able to offer valuable help and advice at almost every step of your APBT ownership. A friend who is experienced with this breed will be in an excellent and objective position to view the overall external physical condition of your pet. Be certain that your "experienced breeder" really knows what he or she is talking about. Also, it is important that your breed expert fully understand that your APBT is your family pet and not just another dog, from a multiple-dog setting, that may not have close contact with a family of humans.

The Veterinarian

While you and the family are the major molding force in your APBT's health and well-being, and an experienced APBT mentor can be a good source of information, it will be your veterinarian who will play the key role in your dog's health plan. No one should be more knowledgeable or better prepared in how to keep your APBT in good shape or to get it back into good shape in the event of a health issue or health problem.

Choosing a veterinarian for your APBT is an important decision. Most veterinary practitioners are skillful, caring professionals who offer sound care and treatment to their animal patients and solid information and guidance to their patient's owners. For your APBT, you may want just a little more. The health needs of certain breeds are somewhat different from the needs of most other dogs. Try to find a veterinarian who not only has had positive experience with APBTs or Amstaffs, but likes these dogs as well. Many veterinarians know that the APBT has gotten a bad rap. You want to be certain that your veterinarian feels comfortable with this breed and understands, among other things, the dog's high tolerance of pain.

Preventive Care

Prevention is always to be preferred over treatment; where you can have a preventive focus, you should. Preventing health problems for a tough and sometimes misunderstood breed involves several diverse aspects of APBT ownership.

From the Start

Wise choosing: Choosing an APBT from physically and temperamentally sound stock is an essential element in an effort to avoid some painful, expensive, and heart-rending circumstances later. No dog can be absolutely guaranteed to not develop serious medical problems during its life. Choosing a puppy or an adult APBT with a potentially inheritable medical problem in its pedigree increases the likelihood of problems in this generation as well.

Training: Failing to prepare adequately for a rapidly maturing, powerful, and sometimes aggressive dog increases the probability of accidents and possible dire consequences. For example, assuming that your APBT will always be a model canine citizen and never get into trouble when running free in a neighborhood is ludicrous and a recipe for disaster. If you don't have your dog under some form of control or restraint at all times outside—a fence, a leash, combined with good training—serious medical, legal, and public perception problems are certain to come your dog's way.

Nutrition: Because of the demand placed on the metabolism, bones, and muscle tissue of a rapidly growing APBT, owners must become well versed in dog nutrition generally and in APBT nutrition specifically. Failure to do so can result in an adult APBT that doesn't reach its full genetic potential.

Regular medical care: Regular physical examinations by a licensed veterinary practitioner will not only identify and treat many existing medical conditions, but will also spot other potential problems that can be avoided with preventive care. No dog should go without immunizations and regular checkups.

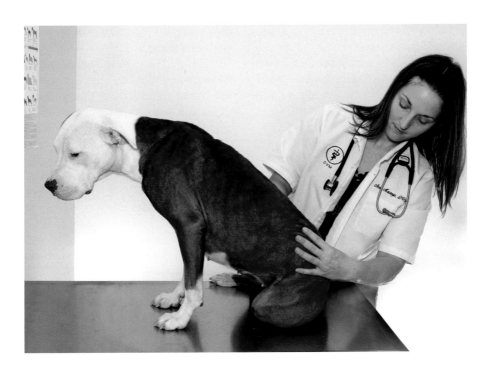

Readiness attitude: Hoping for the best while preparing for the worst is a sound philosophy for a novice APBT owner. Even with the best of care, feeding, medical attention, training, and a safety-oriented environment, a puppy or an adult dog can sometimes become injured or sick. While having a good working relationship with an APBT-aware veterinarian is part of an emergency plan, there are other factors that must be considered:

1. You may need help getting your sick or injured pet to the veterinary office. Not everyone will be willing or able to provide this help on the spur of the moment. Plan for just such circumstances, hoping that they will never occur.

2. Knowledge of possible APBT-threatening conditions, such as gastric torsion or bloat (see page 151) is a mandatory precondition before becoming the owner of an APBT. Knowing about these conditions, certain preventives, and what to do if such problems arise must be part of any prevention plan.

Immunizations

Your APBT may come from a long line of battlers, but against the most dangerous foes it will ever face, your APBT will need a lot of expert help. Not only are inoculations a part of your APBT's preventive health plan, in most places some of these illness-fighting shots are required by law.

Your APBT puppy probably had its first immunizations at about six weeks of age while still at the breeder. These initial shots were vaccinations for distemper, and possibly parvovirus, canine hepatitis, leptospirosis, parainfluenza, coronavirus, and bordetella.

This initial round of inoculations does not complete your pup's immunization needs. In order to prevent these diseases, a series of follow-up shots are given usually at eight to ten weeks, again at twelve weeks, and finally at sixteen to eighteen weeks. Rabies inoculations are given between three and six months of age. Regular rabies boosters,

depending on the rules of your state, are also needed.

Your APBT puppy's immunization record should be made a part of the permanent records that you get when you buy the puppy; this would also be true if you obtain an adult dog. Your veterinarian needs to know what vaccinations (or any other treatments) your dog has received before you became his owner. This complete listing of what has been done to and for your APBT is the basis of your pet's health records. These records are very important. They should be accurate and kept up to date.

Your veterinarian will set up a vaccination schedule. Your job is seeing that your young APBT is on hand to get these immunizations that form the foundation of illness prevention. If you are careless or lackadaisical about this important task, you probably should never have brought a puppy into your life, and certainly not an APBT puppy!

Distemper

Canine distemper (CD) has a long history of dealing tragically with many kinds of animals, especially dogs. Once the deadliest disease-enemy of puppies and young dogs, distemper has been brought under control, but still exists in some places and under some conditions. This extremely infectious and widely spread viral disease raged through kennels many years ago and would kill most of the young dogs and all of the puppies. So devastating was the impact of distemper that some kennels were never able to recover. In some countries, entire dog populations were threatened and some localized breeds pushed to the edge of extinction.

Veterinary science has developed an immunization program that has greatly lowered the number of cases of this dread killer, but the inoculations only work if they are given at the right time and followed by annual boosters. In places where dogs aren't adequately vaccinated, distemper still occurs. This disease is still a big killer in feral canine and other wild animal populations.

Canine distemper is primarily a disease of the brain and can be spread without physical contact, by canine vectors. Spread may be incidental, by unknowing humans who handle CD infected puppies and then touch a healthy, unimmunized dog. Various other means of transmission could include airborne spread through sneezes from infected animals. A dog that has not been immunized can begin to show clinical signs of distemper as soon as a week after being infected with distemper. Initially, distemper appears as a cold with a runny nose and a low fever. In most cases, the dog "goes off its feed" or simply stops eating altogether. Listlessness, fatigue, and diarrhea are observed in most dogs. Veterinary medical science has done much to eliminate distemper from the lives of dogs and dog owners. Vaccination and yearly booster shots have made this killer of puppies and young dogs much less of a threat. Your APBT deserves a better fate than betting his life against distemper.

Rabies

Very few diseases evoke the level of fear that rabies, the dreaded "madness" of hydrophobia, can. Mental pictures of once-faithful dogs turning into mouth-foaming, raging monsters is still entrenched deep in the minds of people who remember when most pets were not inoculated against this infectious, fatal disease.

The saliva of an infected animal through bite wounds usually transmits rabies. Most warm-blooded mammals, including human beings, can be victims of rabies, but it is most often spread through skunks, bats, raccoons, foxes, horses, cows, unvaccinated cats and dogs, and other small animals.

In some places, rabies is relatively widespread. Other areas, like England, have effectively eradicated rabies largely through a widespread prevention program and strict quarantine restrictions. Until 1885, when Louis Pasteur developed the first vaccine against rabies, this disease meant certain death. Before its fatal outcome, rabies would present certain classic signs. The first of these was the symptom that gave the disease the descriptive name— hydrophobia—"a fear of water." The rabies virus infection causes paralysis of muscles that control swallowing. In later stages of the disease, the victim is unable to swallow; salivation is excessive, which leads to the miscalled term, "foaming at the mouth," a well known warning sign of the disease. The infected mammal would be unable and "afraid" to drink water or eat anything. Two phases also were usually seen: the furious phase when the animal would attack anything and everything around it and in which the infected animal died, and the next phase, the dumb or more inactive stage that ends in paralysis, coma, and death.

Your APBT is a powerful and generally active dog. There have been many APBT-bashing jokes over the past several years that referred to "pit bulls with rabies." While these remarks were usually attempts at sick humor, a very valid threat underlies these jokes. Rabies in such powerful, agile, and athletic animals would represent a significant threat to you, your family, and others. Immunization at three to six months, with another inoculation at the age of one year followed by regular rabies shots thereafter will protect your APBT from this horrible and now so unnecessary death.

Leptospirosis

Leptospirosis is a disease that primarily damages the kidneys. It is commonly spread by drinking or coming into contact with water contaminated by the urine of an infected animal. Clinical signs of leptospirosis are: bloody urine (hematuria), loss of appetite, fever, vomiting and diarrhea, and abdominal pain.

Left untreated, this disease can severely damage the liver and the kidneys. Leptospirosis can result in jaundice, weakened hindquarters, mouth sores, and weight loss. Immunization for leptospirosis and annual booster shots are usually enough to protect your APBT.

Hepatitis

Though not the disease of the same name that affects human beings, infectious canine hepatitis (IHC or CAV-1 infection) is quite a serious illness of dogs and puppies. Hepatitis can be caught by any member of the canine family and can be contracted by dogs at any age. Cases of hepatitis can range from a relatively mild sickness to a rapidly progressing viral infection that can take the life of the infected dog within 24 hours of the onset of the illness.

Clinical signs of infectious canine hepatitis can include listlessness, fever, blood in stools and vomitus, abdominal pain, light sensitivity of the eyes, and tonsillitis. Hepatitis, as an infectious disease, is often spread by contact with the feces or urine of an infected animal. Immunization with a yearly booster is a reliable preventive measure.

Parvovirus

Parvovirus (often shortened to "parvo") is another serious killer, especially of puppies, but it can mean death to an unvaccinated or untreated dog at any age. Parvovirus primarily attacks the bone marrow, immune system, and gastrointestinal tract, but can also damage the heart. Puppies with

parvovirus can suffer from severe dehydration because of profuse bloody, watery diarrhea and vomiting and may die within 48 hours after the onset of the disease. If your unimmunized APBT puppy were to encounter a parvovirus-infected dog, humans that have handled an infected animal, or even airborne vectors, a debilitating disease with potentially fatal consequences could result.

While good veterinary care can save some parvovirus victims, immunization is a much better course of action. Puppy vaccination followed by annual follow-up shots should keep your pet safe from parvovirus.

Parainfluenza

Parainfluenza is a highly infectious viral disease than can rapidly spread through a kennel or home where several dogs live. Parainfluenza is spread by contact with infected animals, their surroundings, and aerosol means of transmission—through the air, from sneezes and coughs of infected animals. This viral disease often causes an attending illness called tracheobronchitis, which is usually identified by a dry, hacking cough followed by retching in an attempt to cough up mucus. In and of itself, parainfluenza is not usually a serious illness. Untreated, however, tracheobronchitis can weaken a dog and make it vulnerable to other ailments and infections, especially pneumonia

Parainfluenza is preventable by vaccination in the puppy series with annual booster shots. A veterinarian best provides treatment for this dis-

ease, with the patient isolated from other dogs to decrease the chances of further contagion.

Bordetella

Bordetella is a bacterial infection often found in association with parainfluenza that in turn causes tracheobronchitis. The presence of bordetella may make treatment of tracheobronchitis more difficult. Keep your APBT safe from this infectious disease (and its "fellow travelers") by immunizing against it.

Coronavirus

This contagious disease, which can cause severe diarrhea with watery, loose, foul-smelling, bloody stools, can affect dogs of any age. Coronavirus is similar to parvovirus in that related maladies could leave

a dog or puppy in such a weakened condition that other infections are more easily contracted.

Coronavirus treatment by your veterinarian can be successful, but prevention by immunization is preferred. Prevention is always better than treatment. A good immunization program should allow you the opportunity to avoid putting your pet at risk for some of the more serious medical problems and side effects.

Other Medical Problems

Borelliosis (Lyme Disease)

Borelliosis or Lyme disease is a serious, potentially fatal disease that affects warm-blooded animals and humans. Since your APBT may walk in the park or any wooded area, the possibility of exposure to Lyme disease must be considered. This ailment could even be contracted in your pet's own backyard.

Lyme disease was first identified in Lyme, Connecticut, and is spread primarily by the deer tick, a tiny little bloodsucker credited with carrying an illness that can do your APBT, and *you*, great physical harm. Borelliosis, the medical name for this disease, can affect your dog in several ways, but usually a swelling and tenderness around the joints is observable. It has been shown that the length of time a Lyme disease-carrying tick stays embedded is directly related to the likelihood of developing Lyme disease. Speed in discovering the presence of, and then removing the tick, is highly recommended. If you find a tick on your dog, or suspect that a tick has bitten the dog, immediate removal of the tick (see page 156) and prompt veterinary care for the dog is advisable.

If you have been bitten by a tick, or evidence the telltale tick bite with its characteristic surrounding red area—somewhat like a bull's-eye on a target—take the same action, and contact your own physician or county health department. In both cases, yours and the dog's, timely diagnosis and treatment are essential.

Ridding your yard of ticks is a good idea. Your local health department and your exterminator can be of help in cutting down the chances of a Lyme disease-carrying tick bit-

ing your American Pit Bull Terrier right in his own backyard.

Bloat/Gastric Torsion

Bloat or gastric torsion is a very serious health concern for all of the large, deep-chested breeds of dogs, which includes the APBT. Bloat, which has been known to painfully kill an otherwise healthy dog in just a few hours, involves a swelling and twisting of the dog's stomach, which becomes distended from gas or water or both. Bloat still remains somewhat of a mystery, with a wide variety of suggested causes that may work independently of one another or in combination. Some of these predisposing factors are:

• A large meal followed by a large intake of water and strenuous exercise.

• A genetic predisposition in some breeds and even within some families within some breeds.

• Agitation at mealtime and stress, brought about by many factors.

• The sex and age of the dog, as males seem to be affected more than females, and dogs over 24 months old are more affected than younger dogs.

• Rapid consumption of a large meal.

• Eating from the ground or floor.

• Hungry dogs being given only one huge meal per day.

Regardless of the causes, bloat remains a real killer of large-breed dogs. Some clinical signs of bloat are:

• Obvious abdominal pain and noticeable abdominal swelling.

• Excessive salivation and rapid breathing.
• Pale and cool-to-the-touch skin in the mouth.
• A dazed and "shocky" look.
• Repeated attempts to vomit, especially when nothing comes up.

A dog with bloat needs immediate care if it is to stand any chance of survival. Don't panic; call your veterinarian, and then safely transport your APBT *immediately* to the clinic.

Hip Dysplasia

Hip dysplasia, or HD, is another major canine health problem. While it does not have the usually fatal consequences of gastric torsion, HD can be quite painful and debilitating. It is a medical condition in which the hip joint is slack or loose, combined with a deformity of the socket of the hip and the femoral head joining the thighbone. Malformed development of the hip's connecting tissues leaves an unstable hip joint. Instead of being a stable fitting for the end of the thighbone, the HD-affected hip socket is usually quite shallow. HD can cause a wobbling, unsteady gait, which can be very painful.

HD is inherited, but it must be acknowledged that not every puppy produced by dysplastic parents will have HD itself. It is also true that occasional nondysplastic parents will produce some dysplastic puppies.

HD cannot always be diagnosed until a puppy is more than two years old. The Orthopedic Foundation for Animals (OFA) has developed a widely used X-ray method of determining the presence or absence of HD. You should get an APBT puppy from a mating in which both parents have been tested and certified for this condition. This can reduce the chances of your pup having this painful malady.

Diarrhea and Vomiting

Some diarrhea and vomiting is the result of ordinary events such as changes in food or some added stress, and in puppies, vomiting and diarrhea can also be commonly caused by internal parasites. However, both diarrhea and vomiting can be early warning signals of more serious ailments.

Any extended period (more than 12 to 24 hours) of vomiting or diarrhea should alert you to the need for a quick trip to the veterinarian. Even if this early alarm is a false one, the next one may not be.

Anal Sac Impaction

The anal sacs lie just under the skin on each side of the anus. Normally, these sacs, filled with oily secretions, are emptied naturally when the dog defecates. When the openings to these sacs become stopped up or impacted, the sacs must be emptied by hand of their strong-smelling secretions. One sign of impacted anal sacs is when a dog scoots along the floor dragging its rear end. Your veterinarian can empty the anal sacs or can show you how to do this yourself.

Note: Almost every breed of dog will have one or more conditions that are passed along genetically from generation to generation. A tendency toward bloat or hip dysplasia could be examples of just such inherited conditions. When purchasing a young APBT, you should be aware of any health problems within the line and avoid an APBT that comes from stock with the more serious problems that repeatedly occur in following generations.

Internal Parasites

Dogs and puppies often have worms, parasites that draw their sustenance from your pet and can lead to some serious health problems. Through some simple tests, your veterinarian can detect the presence of worms, and can also prescribe an appropriate drug treatment and eradication program that will lead to their elimination. Let your veterinarian treat your APBT for worms. Even though various worm treatments are available on the market, your dog's doctor will best know how to treat your pet for these parasites in the most effective and safest manner.

Annual or biannual veterinarian examinations will catch most parasites; however, if you find that your APBT has a parasitic infestation, go immediately and don't wait until your APBT's next regular scheduled check. Early diagnosis of parasites can help lessen the negative impact these interlopers can have on your APBT's overall health.

Worms are usually discovered by examination of your dog's stools or by blood sample. The most common worms affecting dogs are: round-worms, hookworms, tapeworms, and heartworms. Each of these parasites must be treated specifically by your veterinarian.

Roundworms

Puppies are the most common targets of roundworms, even though dogs of all ages can have a roundworm infestation. An infected mother dog can pass these parasites along to her offspring prenatally so that it is highly possible for some puppies to have roundworms even before they are born.

Roundworms sap a puppy's vitality; young APBTs with round-worms will not thrive. A healthy puppy should have a clearly healthy appearance. Roundworms take that appearance away. A pendulous abdomen or potbelly may look cute (to a person who doesn't know dogs) on a puppy, but such condi-

tions are also possible indicators of roundworms. Puppies with round-worms may pass their eggs, or in heavy infestations, adult worms, in their stools. Adult roundworms can also be seen in vomitus. Recognize that roundworms sap the vim and vigor and the overall health of your APBT puppy and reduce its growth rate. If you discover roundworms, don't delay, get your puppy to a vet-erinarian to rid him of the health-robbing parasites.

Practice good kennel hygiene to prevent roundworm infestation. Keep all puppy places very clean and sani-tary. Quickly and appropriately dis-pose of all stools.

Hookworms

Hookworms can strike dogs at any age, but they really have a negative impact on puppies. Pup-pies infested with hookworms will have bloody or tarlike stools. As with roundworms, such puppies can also fail to thrive. Hookworm-infested puppies don't eat properly and fail to keep their weight. Since hookworms are actually tiny vampires that attach themselves to the insides of the small intestines and literary suck blood, they can rapidly reduce a puppy to a greatly weakened state. A conse-quence of hookworms in puppies is anemia, which can be fatal.

Trust your veterinarian to make your puppy hookworm free and on the road to health. As with so many other conditions and parasites, ken-nel hygiene is a definite part of a successful prevention plan.

Tapeworms

Fleas that have tapeworms are the vectors that put these parasites into your dog's system. Tapeworms, in modest numbers usually don't cause severe harm to a dog, but these flat, segmented parasites do pull down your dog's overall health. A dog with tapeworms cannot be truly healthy. For your APBT to grow into its full potential, tapeworms must be eradicated from your pet. This will also usually mean destroy-ing the external parasites that brought the internal parasites

Consult your veterinarian about a treatment plan for the elimination of tapeworms. Also ask about how to do away with the delivery sys-tem that brought its parasite to your pet—the flea (see page 155). The elimination of a recurrent tapeworm infestation is just another good rea-son for also eliminating fleas from your dog's life.

Heartworms

Another parasite of a parasite, the heartworm comes to your pet from its transport or intermediate host, the mosquito. A heartworm-infected mosquito bites your dog and deposits the heartworm larvae onto your pet's skin. The larvae enter the hole made by the mosquito into the bloodstream and ultimately to the heart.

Heartworm larvae-infected mos-quitoes are ready to share their ever-present threat in an ever-expanding area of this country. Heartworm dis-ease presently exists in most of the country. Left untreated, heartworms will cause heart failure and certainly lead to a premature death.

Your veterinarian can help you with a plan to prevent heartworm infection. This involves regular testing and administering of medicine to kill heartworm larvae in circulation *before* they enter the heart. It must be given to a dog that does not yet have an adult heartworm infection.

Treatment for adult heartworms is a long, risky, and expensive procedure. Prevention is, by far, a better course of action and could save your APBT from an early and miserable death.

External Parasites

Fleas

Fleas are the bane of many a dog's life. They are the most common external parasite afflicting dogs and they feed on your APBT's blood. In extreme cases, fleas can cause anemia in your dog and, in almost all cases, make a dog's life miserable. Fleas add insult to injury in that not only are they an external parasite, but they harbor and introduce the internal parasite—the tapeworm— into your dog. Some dogs, like some humans, can have an extreme allergic reaction to flea bites. *Flea bite allergy* makes its victim suffer far more than a nonallergic dog. This allergy can cause hair loss, skin infections, and incessant scratching. Immediate attention by a veterinarian and diligent flea control by the owner are required to alleviate this extremely uncomfortable condition.

Dealing with fleas involves a "take charge and take no prisoners" mentality. The sooner you realize that it is an all-out war between you and the fleas, the sooner you can begin to attack these little parasites in *every* place they live. If your dog has fleas, every place the dog goes will have fleas—its bed, the yard, the kennel, the car, and your home.

Failure to hit your flea enemy in any one of these battlefields—and probably several others that you can name—is as good as a complete failure. If fleas can survive in the yard, merely getting them out of the house is only a temporary victory; they will be back in your house in no time.

By consulting with your veterinarian and perhaps someone in the pet supply business you should be able to obtain a variety of weapons in your flea war. Flea dips, flea shampoos, flea powder, flea collars, and flea sprays are all on-dog remedies. Their use should be coordinated by a call to your veterinarian and be based on the knowledge that fleas spend 90 percent of their life cycle *off* your dog. Only the adult fleas, about 10 percent of the population of fleas, are on your dog.

To take care of the 90 percent of the life cycle of fleas that inhabit your yard, your car, your couch, and so forth, you must use other products. Consult with your exterminator about how to handle fleas off the dog. Always use flea killers with

great care and follow their directions implicitly!

Ticks

Ticks are another external parasite that can make a dog's life more uncomfortable. Like fleas, ticks also live on the host's blood. Because ticks are much larger than fleas, they suck more blood and can actually increase their size several hundred percent—all at the expense of your dog.

Although ticks are always a nuisance, they also carry life-threatening disease (see Lyme Disease, page 150). They can also cause infected sores and scars on your APBT if the ticks are removed incorrectly. Not only are these sores pain-

ful, but because of the APBT's short coat, they are unsightly.

Ticks can be controlled with the regular use of veterinarian-recommended on-dog sprays or dips, and living area treatments. It is important to remember to wear rubber gloves when removing a tick from your APBT, in case the tick is a Lyme disease carrier. Try not to leave part of the tick's mouthparts in your dog's skin, which can lead to infection. To remove ticks follow these steps:

1. Place a small amount of rubbing alcohol at the exact site of the tick bite. Be careful that the dog doesn't get any of this denatured alcohol into his mouth or eyes.

2. After making certain that the pet will remain still, use tweezers to grab the tick as close to the dog's skin as possible, pulling VERY slowly on the tick's head and mouth.

3. Try to get the entire tick from of your APBT's skin.

4. Put additional alcohol or another antiseptic on the bite.

5. Dispose of the tick by dropping the tick into a cup or container filled with alcohol so that it will not get back on your dog or onto you.

6. Sometimes you will see two ticks at one bite site, a large blood-engorged one (the female) and a small, often dark brown one (the male). Be sure to get BOTH ticks out of your APBT's skin.

Ticks like to get into an APBT's evidently tick-inviting ears. Always check your dog over carefully after any trips to the woods or to a park where ticks might be, or even the backyard.

Ear Mites

The ears (trimmed or untrimmed) of your APBT can also be targets of another bothersome pest, the ear mite. These microscopic mites live in the ear canal. Mite infestations can cause a dark, dirty, waxy material to adhere to the inner skin of the ears. These ear mites can cause dogs a great deal of discomfort, as evidenced by excessive ear scratching and violent head shaking.

Your APBT's veterinarian is your best line of defense against this parasitic invader. Regularly inspect your dog's ears. If you suspect ear mites, seek professional help with these pests, which are usually transmit-ted through contact with infested animals.

Mange

There are several types of mange, caused by mites:

Red, or demodectic mange: This type of mange especially affects physically vulnerable pets, such as young puppies or oldsters, causing ragged, patchy hair loss sometimes accompanied by severe itching;

Sarcoptic mange: (Also known as "scabies") This ailment comes from a type of mite that burrows into the dog's outer layers of skin. Scabies causes a great deal of hair loss and intense itching. This kind of mange doesn't stay only with pets; it can also be transmitted to pet owners.

These and other types of mange can make your APBT uncomfortable and unsightly and unhealthy. Let your veterinarian provide a treatment and eradication program.

Skin Problems

APBTs may develop other skin problems. These might be fungal, allergic, or stress-related. Even the color of your APBT may be a partial reason for these conditions. Blue and dilute-colored dogs, in other breeds as well as APBTs, are more predisposed to skin problems than their fawn, black, or brindle peers. Some pet foods contribute to rashes or "hot spots," as some dogs definitely seem allergic to some food ingredients.

First Aid Kit

Ask your veterinarian about things needed in a first aid kit for your APBT. Such kits are available from some of the larger pet product retailers. You should have a kit readily available in your home, which you should always take with you on extended trips. Your kit can be kept in a satchel or fishing tackle box and should include items such as:

• extra collar and leash
• baby wipes in a resealable package
• hydrogen peroxide (3%)
• antiseptic powder or ointment (as recommended by your veterinarian)
• scissors
• tweezers or hemostat
• thermometer
• iodine or Mercurochrome (as recommended by your veterinarian)
• two containers of bottled water
• APBT-sized muzzle
• canine first aid guide
• bandaging materials: cotton, elastic pressure bandages, adhesive tape
• breaking stick
• copies of your pet's medical information

The question of skin problems and poor coat quality may be a classic "nature or nurture" conflict, Where you purchase your APBT and its family or strain will play a great part in whether your dog has skin problems or problem skin. You can avoid some skin problems by wisely choosing the right puppy from the right breeder. You can also prevent some skin difficulties by the kind of care you give your APBT. Good housekeeping and regular inspections of your pet's coat can catch "hot spot" problems and parasites before they have a deleterious effect on your APBT. Working on this problem with your veterinarian, not only for after-the-fact treatment, but before skin problems occur will make such skin problems less likely.

Emergency Care for Your APBT

The Team Approach

As mentioned earlier, when discussing the prevention team for your APBT's care, you will also need an emergency team to help you if your pet has an injury or immobilizing sickness. Because people perceive your pet as a "pit bull," some may be reluctant to help you take a sick or injured dog to the veterinarian. You may be able to get someone from the police, fire, or sheriff's department to come out and give you a hand in getting your pet to medical care.

Note: Remember always that you have a dog that sometimes brings out the worst in some people. If your pet has been in a fight and is injured, be certain that you aren't arrested and your dog impounded because it may be seen as a "pit fighting dog."

Some veterinarians may make house calls but in an emergency, this may not be a possible or logical alternative. Always ask your veterinarian what to do in transporting a sick or injured dog. Because veterinarians deal with such issues all the time, they may have options and alternatives you might not realize.

Accidents

Even though you have diligently tried to be the best dog-owners, and even though you have done well with preventive care, training, and control, accidents will happen. When they do, you must be prepared.

Though your pet may be from one of the least human-aggressive breeds on the planet, the first rule in dealing with an injured canine is: *Don't make things worse!* Rough handling can turn a simple fracture into a compound fracture, an injured back into paralysis. As you assess the injury to your pet, try to do so with a clear head. This dog may mean the world to you, but if you really want to help your pet, you must act rationally. Some of the smart moves to make around an injured pet are:

• Speak in a calm and reassuring voice to allay the fears of your frightened pet.

• Always approach any injured animal slowly and deliberately, even if the pet and you have been best friends for years. Speed may be important, but too much rushing around can actually slow down the emergency-aid process; your dog will pick up on any hysteria that your voice or demeanor conveys and be even more frightened.

• Gently but securely muzzle the dog; an APBT-sized muzzle might be a good item for the first aid kit.

• If a regular muzzle isn't available, use a necktie, a belt, a leash, or something similar.

• To avoid further injury put the dog on a makeshift stretcher such as a tabletop, a sturdy piece of plywood, or even a strong tarpaulin. One person should place both hands on the dog as the stretcher is lifted, securing the dog so it won't fall or jump off.

• Attend to any immediate bleeding (see Bleeding, on page 160).

• Call your veterinarian to alert him or her that you are on your way and will need help getting into the clinic.

• Drive *safely* to the clinic; don't aggravate your APBT's injuries or endanger yourself by reckless driving.

Many of the most serious injuries to pets, even powerful APBTs, occur when an automobile strikes a dog. It is extremely unwise to allow an APBT to run free and unrestrained in the community. The potential for dog fights is one reason; being killed or seriously injured in an uneven confrontation with a car or truck is another. Always be especially alert in any situations where your dog could run out into a street or highway.

Heatstroke

Your APBT may die a miserable death in a matter of only a few minutes if left inside an automobile with poor ventilation and high inside temperatures. This totally unnecessary and preventable death can happen in a short time on any sunny day; it doesn't have to be a hot summer day. Any time when the weather is only moderately warm, 60°F (15.6°C) or higher, can be fatal. *Never* put your dog in such a senselessly dangerous and potential fatal situation!

Clinical signs of heatstroke include a dazed look and rapid, shallow panting with a high fever. The dog's gums will appear bright red. Time is of extreme importance. You must act *immediately*, even before going to the nearest veterinarian. Lower the dog's temperature by pouring cool water or a mixture of cool water and alcohol over the dog, before heading to the animal hospital.

Bleeding

If your APBT is bleeding, identify the source of the blood and apply firm but gentle pressure over the area with your hand. If the injury is on an extremity, apply pressure to the wound to stop the bleeding. Continued bleeding, any significant blood loss, or a gaping wound will require veterinary attention. Treat any bleeding as a serious situation worthy of your immediate attention!

Poisoning

Your APBT, sometimes just because it *is* an APBT, is at risk in a number of ways, but never more so than in its own home and yard from accidental poisoning. We live in a chemical-laden society. In practically any home there are any many toxic materials that your pet could accidentally lick or eat. Some of the most dangerous and lethal poisons are things that we normally have around the house and use every day. Some of the most common toxic agents around the average dog's home include:

• Antifreeze, which is a deadly poison to pets; it has a sweet taste than many dogs love. Dogs and cats will readily lap up spills and leaks.

• Chocolate, which, in sufficient amounts, can kill even a tough and powerful dog like your APBT.

• A number of outside plants that are dangerous, especially to a young APBT still in the chewing stages. Such landscaping standards as azalea, rhododendron, holly, and other

yard plants can be deadly. Even wild plants, such as mistletoe and poison ivy, have been known to cause severe reactions in dogs. Check with your *local* county extension service for a listing of deadly plants that are either widely planted or that grow wild in your geographical area.

• Some houseplants that can also be killers. Even popular flowers and plants such as dieffenbachia, poinsettia, and jade plants can be deadly.

• Some household cleaners, which can also kill an inquisitive pet. Keep all solvents, insecticides, pesticides, and cleaners away from your APBT and its environment.

Note: If your dog suddenly begins to act listless, has convulsions, or acts disoriented, it may have been poisoned. Other signs include diarrhea, vomiting, and a change in color of the mucous membranes. If you see these signs, rush your pet to the veterinarian.

If Your APBT Is in a Dogfight

To ignore the possibility that your APBT may become embroiled in a fight is to neglect rational thinking. There are some steps that you can take to avoid a fight, and some things to do after a fight has occurred:

• Always keep your pet under control.

• If your APBT is animal-aggressive and you feel it advisable to walk the dog in public places, get a strong leash and collar, invest in a strong muzzle, or perhaps a head harness, and use all three.

• Avoid other dogs and other people with other dogs, if your dog is likely to act up.

• Invest in some training with a professional to quell the aggressive behavior.

• Always carry a "breaking stick" with you. (A breaking stick is a chisel-shaped piece of wood or plastic that you can use to wedge into your APBT's jaws to make it let loose whatever it has gripped.) In the event a breaking stick is needed:

1. Use care in straddling your pet (watch the other dog more than your own).

2. Try to immobilize your dog, using your body weight to do so.

3. Grab the dog's neck and turn the neck to expose the point of the gripping bite.

4. Edge the breaking stick into the dog's mouth, immediately behind the incisors and in front of the molars.

5. Twist the breaking stick to make the dog release its grip and open its mouth.

6. Keep the gripping stick in place to prevent the dog from going for another hold.

7. Back the dog away.

Note: Breaking up any dog fight is difficult and dangerous to the person attempting to do the breaking. Breaking up a fight between an American Pit Bull Terrier and a dog of another breed is harder because the other dog may bite *you*. Breaking up a fight between two APBTs requires two strong people, two breaking sticks, and a large amount of guts and luck. *It must be done!* You can't sit back and hope that the dogs will stop fighting on their own. The APBT won't stop. You must do the stopping.

Giving Your APBT Medicine

You should know how to give your APBT the medicines prescribed by the dog's veterinarian for treatment or disease-prevention purposes. Some dogs simply don't like to take medicine and will spit out pills and capsules. Some experienced dog medicine givers hide the pill or capsule in a dog treat, such as bread covered with canned dog food or a small glob of peanut butter, or perhaps a little clump of semi-moist food with the medicine hidden inside.

Other dog people take the more direct approach of opening the dog's mouth, slightly leaning its head back a short way, and then placing the pill as far back on the dog's tongue as they can reach. They then simply close the dog's mouth, speaking calmly and wait for the dog to swallow.

Liquid medicine is administered in a similar way to pills and capsules. Remembering to keep the head back only a little way, simply pour the medicine over the back of the tongue. Speak soothingly as you close the APBT's mouth and wait for the dog to swallow.

Always faithfully follow the veterinarian's dosages and instructions carefully. Never use outdated medicines or give your APBT medication designed for humans or other animals without advance approval from your dog's veterinarian.

Old Age and the APBT

One day that sturdy APBT puppy will grow up. Barring unforeseen fatal accidents or injuries, an APBT could spend 12 or 15 years as a part of your family, but one day, your trusted pet will become a gray-muzzled senior. Even though this is a very hardy breed, your treatment of your pet must now be different. The old APBT will sleep a little more; its play will be a little less vigorous. The oldster will still love you and the other members of its family, and will still want to be included; it just can't go as fast as before.

It is important to remember that even if your pet is old, it is still an APBT. If you have been conscientious in protecting your pet from potential fights with other dogs since it was a puppy, don't stop now. Many incidents in the annals of fighting dog lore tell how long-retired dogs were severely injured or killed when their owners forgot to continue vigilance in keeping dogs apart. If your APBT was animal-aggressive earlier in its life, there is no reason to believe that age will dim this inborn trait. Always be protective, even of an old dog.

A whole new set of issues will be important now. Your APBT may need a dog food for senior canines. Its teeth and gums will need extra care. There may be some hearing loss and possible eye problems. Most of these issues can be handled by timely visits to the veterinarian and by your ongoing attention to the changing needs of your pet.

Teeth

Your APBT will need good dental care all of its life. As a terrier with very strong jaws (no stronger than many other large and powerful dogs may have, contrary to popular myth) that it has used for aggressive chewing all its life, the teeth will need special care in the older dog. Tartar accumulation can bring on gum and tooth disease. You can lessen tartar and also greatly insure good dental health for your dog by regularly inspecting your APBT's teeth and gums, not only for tartar, but for signs of tooth decay and foreign objects, usually pieces of wood from the dog's chewing on sticks and so forth, cleaning your APBT's teeth at home, regular veterinary dental checkups with occasional teeth cleanings by experienced veterinary staff members, and the use of veterinarian-approved chew toys and dental exercisers, designed to help remove tartar and plaque.

Eyes

The APBT's eyes will need continued attention as the dog ages. Other than the puppy-proofing and APBT-proofing that should have long been a part of your regular regimen, you need to protect your old dog from sharp objects that might be just at eye level. You also need to keep the APBT safe from toxic substances or fumes that can irritate or damage eyes.

Neighborhood children throwing stones or shooting an air rifle at what is called the "pit bull" in the neighborhood could do your APBT damage. Air pollution, thorny plants, and heavy underbrush all have eye-damaging potential. Even aging itself could bring on such problems as cataracts. All of these eye problems can be greatly lessened in severity by regular eye inspections performed by you and by your veterinarian during general checkups.

You may notice some mucus collecting in the corners of your APBT's eyes from time to time. This is usually a perfectly normal condition that can be simply removed by gentle wiping with a soft cloth; however, don't confuse this ordinary clear mucouslike material with a yellowish or bloody eye discharge that can signal an eye problem and that requires professional attention.

Ears

Whether your APBT has had its ears cropped as many show dogs do, or whether your dog has its ears in their natural state, these ears will need regular attention and ongoing care from you. If you have a rescue dog, or if your APBT has gotten into a scrap at some time in his life, the ears may have rends and tears from fighting. Dog ears are among the favorite hiding places of such parasites as ticks and ear mites (See Ticks, page 156 and Ear mites, page 157). Regular inspection of the ears will let you spot these parasites and you will need a plan to exterminate them.

Sometimes a male dog's ears will be a record of the hostile interactions it may have had with other male dogs. Also, because of their location high up on either side of the dog's head, ears will take some damage when a big, fast dog runs through underbrush. Always keep a close watch on your pet's ears for cuts or scratches that may need medical attention, yours or the veterinarian's.

Feet and Nails

The feet and nails of most dogs will need special care. Because your APBT is a powerful—and in some strains or families, very large—and athletic dog, he may need even more care. If your pet is engaged in hunting, weight pulls, or other strenuous activities, the potential of a torn nail or an abraded pad is increased. Even a stay-at-home pet APBT can have foot problems. Beginning with good nail and foot care, starting when the APBT is a puppy, is good preventive care. So are regular foot inspections. A third part of a foot care plan would be keeping broken glass and other potentially foot-harming items out of the dog's path. Always remember that the care of an APBT's feet is as important as any other part of the dog's health plan.

APBTs will put a lot of stress on their footpads and on their nails. Regular inspections will let you know if your dog has suffered a slight abrasion that could become a bigger foot problem later. Regular nail trimming is a must for good foot care. You will need a strong set of toenail clippers, either the scissors type or the "guillotine" type and use them regularly as the dog's nails start to grow too long. Remember in nail trimming to keep well away from the "quick" or the main blood supply of the nail. You may have to use an emery board or nail file to shorten nails when the "quick" is too close for easy trimming (see Nail Care, page 102).

The End

One of the most difficult times in the life of any dog owner will be at the end of a good dog's life. More than any other breed, the APBT has been threatened by death throughout the breed's existence. Your pet, whether you want to acknowledge it or not, was often quite near death throughout his life. One instance of past carelessness on your part might have allowed your pet to become another "pit bull" rampaging through a neighborhood. Your pet could have gotten into a fight with another dog and been branded an incorrigible fighter, or even executed by the authorities.

All your life with this pet has been underpinned with your desire and your efforts to keep your APBT safe from harm in a society that seemed determined to destroy it. You took all the early precautions of buying the right puppy from the right source, thoroughly socializing your puppy, carefully training your puppy, providing the right constraints to keep your APBT at home or under your control at all times, avoiding situations where other aggressive dogs (and aggressive dog owners) could start more than they could handle with your dog. You have defended your great APBT from the nasty remarks and glowering stares of a generally ignorant community and sometimes hostile population. You have secretly wept inside when the great pet that is your APBT was branded unjustly, as when mothers crossed the street to avoid you and your pet out on a walk. You have felt the swell of pride when your pet accomplished some difficult feat in obedience, agility, weight pulling, the show ring, or some other special activity. Perhaps your greatest pride came when unbiased people, especially children, hugged and exchanged kisses with your APBT.

Now, after all that you and this good dog have been through together, potentially more than most owners of other dogs would see in the lifetimes of ten dogs, you have to make the ultimately hard decision. When that time comes and you and your veterinarian know it is the right time, handle it as your APBT would: Be tough and gritty and then be willing to let your true love for this pet be measured by the wisdom in knowing when to say good-bye (see Euthanasia, page 101).

Chapter Fifteen

The Pit and the Pendulum

It has been only in the past 30 or so years that this remarkable breed became hated and reviled unjustly. Only a few decades have passed since a little-known breed has become a household word. The APBT has reached heights that Messrs. Bennett, Colby, and McCord would have never dreamed about 100 years ago. That many of those heights have been when the breed was figuratively hung in effigy would have puzzled these men even more. The APBT that they knew was the finest dog they could fashion. It did fight in the pit, but brought none of the pugilist home to the families with children that adored the dogs. The APBT was, as Theodore Roosevelt wrote to his daughter, a great aid to the hunters and ranchers confronted with cougars and lynx.

Helen Keller felt the broad head and short coat of her APBT and loved the stocky animal. Other famous Americans thought nothing of being proud to own such an American original. Stubby, an APBT, held United States Army rank and won medals in World War II and then was belittled and shunned "as a mongrel" by purebred dog people.

The Pendulum Begins to Swing

Today, the American Pit Bull Terrier is recovering some lost ground. More and more people now realize that the "pit bull" is not the APBT. The media is now making a distinction between the types of dogs that have been involved in dog bite cases. One still sees "pit-mix" dogs, but other breeds; Chows, Rottweilers, Dalmatians, Cocker Spaniels, and wolf-dog hybrids are appearing on the weekly list of bites, and fewer and fewer "pit bulls" are seen there. The APBT may have dodged some of the bullets fired at the "pit bull" in the media and in public perception.

Where the APBT continues to lose out is in the halls of justice and the centers of local government. Some municipalities have never had a single incident by an APBT, an American Staffordshire Terrier, or the amusing little Staffordshire Bull Terrier, and yet all three of these breeds generally are right up there with the wolf-dog hybrid and the "pit bull" when banning time rolls around. Most of the politicians who vote on these bans could not identify an APBT, Amstaff, or Staffy Bull with a picture of the three breeds in their hands. Yet ban it they must, and ban it they do.

Recently, there has been a backlash against indiscriminate, wholesale, entire-breed bans. More intelligent elected officials are seeing that breed bans look suspiciously like a canine version of the "Jim Crow" laws. This country has

been there and has done that and doesn't want to go back there.

The Pendulum Swings On

The American Kennel Club practically denied the existence of the APBT for generations. With the advent of breed-specific legislation (see page 74), many of the more astute AKC members are rethinking their position. The APBT, a fighter from the past, is now a show and family dog. Some APBTs are actually in the American Kennel Club as American Staffordshire Terriers. Breed bans rarely affect one breed.

Useful Addresses and Literature

Kennel Clubs

The American Dog Breeders
　Association (ADBA)
P.O. Box 1771
Salt Lake City, UT 84110
www.adbadog.com

The American Kennel Club
260 Madison Avenue
New York, NY 10016
www.akc.org

The United Kennel Club
100 E. Kilgore Road
Kalamazoo, MI 49002
www.ukc.dogs

American Pit Bull Terrier Registry
P.O. Box 1036
Antioch, TN 37011
www.pitbullregistry.com

APBT Activities
Canine Good Citizen (CGC)
See *AKC.org* (the AKC allows
APBTs and other non-AKC dogs to
participate in CGC)

Agility

North American Dog Agility Council
　(NADAC)
P.O. Box 1206
Colbert, OK 74733
www.nadac.com

United Kennel Club has agility
　programs
www.ukc.dogs.

United States Dog Agility
　Association
P.O. Box 850955
Richardson, TX 75085
www.usdaa.com

Behavior and Training
Animal Behavior Society
2611 East 10th Street
Indiana University
Bloomington, IN 47408
www.animalbehavior.org

Association of Pet Dog Trainers
　(APDT)
150 Executive Center Drive
Box 35
Greenville, SC 29615
www.apdt.com

National Association of Dog
   Obedience Instructors (NADOI)
729 Grapevine Hwy.
Hurst, TX 76054
www.nadoi.org

American Temperament Test
   Society
P.O. Box 800130
Balch Springs, TX 75180
www.atts.org

Search and Rescue (many APBTs
excel in this important work)

American Rescue Dog Association,
   Inc.
P.O. Box 613
Bristow, VA 20136
www.ardainc.org

National Association for Search
   and Rescue, Inc.
www.nasar.org

Therapy Dogs (another activity
open to many APBTs)

The Delta Society
289 Perimeter Road – East
Renton, WA 98055
www.deltasociety.com

Therapy Dogs, International, Inc.
88 Bartley Road
Flanders, NJ 07836
www.tdi.dog.org

Weight Pulling
International Weight Pull
   Association (IWPA)
www.iwpa.net

APBT Rescue and Adoption
(There are APBT and pit bull rescue
organizations throughout North
America. Contact the following
organization to find one near you.)

Pit Bull Rescue Central
www.pbrc.net

Magazines
The APBT Gazette
(at the American Dog Breeders
   Association website)
www.adbadog.com

AKC Gazette – Online
www.akc.org

UKC Bloodlines Journal
www.ukc.dogs

Books
General
Coile, D. Caroline, *Encyclopedia
   of Dog Breeds.* Hauppauge,
   New York: Barron's Educational
   Series, Inc., 1998
Coile, D. Caroline, *Show Me! A Dog
   Showing Primer.* Hauppauge,
   New York: Barron's Educational
   Series. Inc., 1997
Millan, Cesar, *Be the Pack Leader:
   Use Cesar's Way to Transform
   Your Dog . . . and Your Life,*
   Harmony Books (Crown
   Publishing), 2007

Millan, Cesar, *A Member of the Family: Cesar Millan's Guide to a Lifetime of Fulfillment with Your Dog,* Harmony Books (Crown Publishing) 2008

Wrede, Barbara. *Civilizing Your Puppy.* Hauppauge, New York: Barron's Educational Series, Inc., 1992

APBT Specific

Duffy, Kyla/Mumford Lowrey, *Lost Souls: Found. Inspiring Stories About Pit Bulls,* Happy Tails Books, 2009

Foster, Ken, *I'm a Good Dog: America's Most Beautiful (and Misunderstood) Pet.* Studio, 2012

Gorant, Jim, *Wallace: The Underdog Who Conquered a Sport, Saved a Marriage and Championed Pit Bulls—One Flying Disc at a Time.* New York, New York: Gotham Books, 2012

Jessup, Diane, *The Working Pit Bull,* Neptune City, New Jersey: TFH Publications, 1995

Stahlkuppe, Joe, *American Pit Bull Terriers and American Staffordshire Terriers.* Hauppauge, New York: Barron's Educational Series, Inc., 2010

Stahlkuppe, Joe, *Training Your Pit Bull,* Hauppauge, New York: Barron's Educational Series, Inc., 2006

Index